Honest to God:

Forty years on

Honest to God: Forty Years On

Edited by
Colin Slee

scm press

© Colin Slee 2004

0 334 02939 2

First published in 2004 by SCM Press
9-17 St Albans Place, London N1 0NX

www.scm-canterburypress.co.uk

SCM Press is a division of
SCM-Canterbury Press Ltd

Printed and bound in Great Britain by
Biddles Ltd, www.biddles.co.uk

Contents

Contents

Foreword

It was a privilege to be asked by Bishop Tom Butler to chair the conference looking at the legacy and continuing influence of John Robinson's book *Honest to God* some 40 years after its publication. When the conference took place in March 2003 I was relatively newly arrived as Bishop of Kingston in Southwark Diocese, but I was aware of its reputation as a place of radical and forward thinking. I was not to be disappointed – either by the conference or by my experience to date. I had lived in the diocese as a teenager and attended an evangelical anglican church which was a deeply formative place for me. I first read *Honest to God* as a sixth former in the early 1970s. I found it a very thought-provoking publication as I wrestled with my own understanding of the nature of God, the incarnation, and the way in which life should be understood and lived as a Christian. It seemed to me then to be asking many of the right questions and attempting to answer them in a manner that would be intelligible to twentieth-century people living in the aftermath of the social and intellectual revolution of the 1960s. If the Christian faith was to remain credible, and if the Church was to survive, it had to engage with these issues.

It was only several years later when I began my theological training that I began to appreciate more fully the scope and vitality of the phenomenon that has been labelled 'South Bank religion', which was centred around the radical thinking of many in Southwark Diocese in the 1960s under the charismatic leadership of Bishop Mervyn Stockwood, and of which *Honest to God* was a notable part. My appreciation of that thinking has been renewed and stimulated since returning to

Southwark in 2002, and not least by the events of the conference from which the papers in this book are taken. I have been
surprised by the number of times people have spoken about
the influence of Bishop Mervyn Stockwood and all that happened under his leadership, including the publication of *Honest
to God*. There is still, 40 years on, an energy and vitality in
the debate that is surprising given the length of time which has
passed and the substantial changes that have occurred in many
areas of South London. One might have expected it to have
disappeared into history. One of the features of the conference
that is etched in my memory is the vision and inspiration felt
by those directly involved in the 1960s. It still shone through
40 years later. Two other aspects of the day also struck me
strongly. The first was a palpable sense of disappointment that
the heady hopes of the 1960s had not been realized as many
would have wished. In several ways life for the Christian faith
and the churches in this country has become more difficult,
both in terms of the numbers of people who actually come to
church and the intellectual climate for the Christian faith. The
second aspect was the continuing ability of *Honest to God* to
provoke keen thought and to ask highly pertinent questions
about both our contemporary understanding of the Christian
faith and the current practices and ways of the Church.

In the planning of the day we tried to reflect the structure
of the book, but to do so in a manner that looked forward
to the contemporary issues facing the Christian faith and the
Church. Our speakers did not disappoint us. There were four
main sessions each of which reflected an aspect of the original
publication. Each session brought together two speakers who
approached the topic from very different angles.

The first session was entitled 'Culture and Context' and we
explored, with the help of Colin Buchanan and Martyn Percy,
Honest to God's attempt to relate doctrine to contemporary
thinking. John Robinson had expressed his concern in the 1960s
that the language of what he called 'supranatural theism' was
making less and less sense to modern people steeped in the
influence of science and the Enlightenment, and the social

upheaval of the 1960s. He spoke of a need to respond to this new context with a 'reluctant revolution' in which we should radically remould our ideas, not least about the very nature of God and the implications of this for our moral thinking.

The second session went under the title 'God-language in *Honest to God* and God-language now'. John Robinson had suggested that metaphors such as the 'Ground of our Being' and 'ultimate depth' were more likely to speak to modern people than much of the traditional language of theism. Christopher Ryan and Don Cupitt explored the question of this need for intelligible language about God. Very sadly Christopher Ryan died suddenly following a short illness in February 2004. He kept up his lively faith and enquiring spirit to the end and we were very grateful and fortunate to be among those who have benefited from his scholarship.

The third session looked at the significance of John Robinson's thinking for the way in which life is to be lived. Under the title 'Belief and Behaviour, God and Goodness – the reduction of religion to ethics?', Trevor Hart (and Peter Gomes via his article) explored the impact of different ways of thinking about God on both worship and prayer and on ethics.

The final session looked at 'The Christology of *Honest to God* and what Jesus means to us today'. John Robinson had questioned the 'entire supranaturalistic frame of reference for Christology' and spoke of Jesus as 'the Man for Others' and as 'the one who is utterly open to and united with the Ground of his Being'. In an ingenious and creative dialogue Jane Williams and Alister McGrath discussed these issues of our understanding of Jesus.

All of the speakers helped to fulfil the overall aim of the conference, which was to use the thinking of *Honest to God* as a springboard for our understanding of God and the Christian faith today, and I would like to express my gratitude to them. I would also thank those chiefly responsible for the conference – the Dean and Chapter of Southwark Cathedral, and notably Canon Jeffrey John; the Bishop of Southwark; and, of course Bishop John Robinson and all those who were originally so engaged with the radical and lively thinking of 'South Bank religion' in the 1960s, which still has the power to stimulate today, 40 years on.

It remains to be seen whether or not the impact of *Honest to God* will really last beyond the lifetimes of those who were directly involved in the 1960s. Our context has changed substantially. In the 1960s modernism and secularism were paramount, but there was still a debate to be had about whether or not the claims of the Christian faith were intelligible and true. In the early twenty-first century we are surrounded by the contours of postmodernism. In a deeply plural culture there is a pervasive relativism that has almost given up on the notion of any common or public 'truth'. We all see the world through different eyes and 'truth' is in the eye of the beholder. So if Christians want to maintain a supernatural understanding of God and Jesus then it is 'true for them'. We do not have to bother about whether or not it makes sense to anyone else. However, such a pervasive relativism will not ultimately do. I would surmise that most people are as suspicious of an easy-going relativism that treats all views as equally valid as they are of a hard-edged fundamentalism that sees only 'my' view of reality as 'the truth'. The questions raised by John Robinson in *Honest to God* 40 years ago are still highly relevant today. We need intelligent, popular theology that explores our understanding of the nature of God and Jesus in a language that connects with people. We need a deep concern for the way in which human life is to be lived and shared. And we need to ask sharp questions about the way in which the Church engages with the society in which it is set. John Robinson played a vital role in stimulating those questions in his day. His legacy is substantial. The challenge for Christians today is to continue to engage with these radical issues in our context. This book is a contribution to that continuing engagement.

Richard Cheetham
Bishop of Kingston

Notes on Contributors

COLIN BUCHANAN was, at the time of the fortieth anniversary of *Honest to God*, Bishop of Woolwich, the fourth in succession following John Robinson. He was ordained in 1961 and was ministering as a curate in Chester diocese in March 1963 at the time of the original publication. While his own major involvement was in issues of liturgy, ecumenism and clergy training, he retained a full library of publications around *Honest to God*, and enjoyed the propriety of the latest Bishop of Woolwich commenting on the bestselling publication of his predecessor. In his own fields he has published extensively, his major book being an evangelical Anglican ecclesiology, *Is the Church of England Biblical?* (DLT, 1998). He was 21 years on the staff of St John's College, Nottingham, and was made bishop in 1985. He was Bishop of Woolwich from 1996 until retiring in July 2004.

RICHARD CHEETHAM is Area Bishop of Kingston in the Diocese of Southwark. After studying physics and philosophy at Oxford University, he began his working life as a science teacher. He was ordained in the Church of England in 1987, and served as a curate in Newcastle upon Tyne. From 1990 he worked as a vicar, and latterly as rural dean in Luton, followed by three and a half years as archdeacon in St Albans. He moved to his current post in October 2002. His research interests centre on understandings of religious belief in contemporary culture, and in 1999 he was awarded a PhD for his research into collective worship in schools.

DON CUPITT is a life fellow of Emmanuel College, Cambridge. After studying theology at Cambridge, where he first got to know John Robinson, he was ordained in 1959 and served a curacy in the north of England before returning to Cambridge in 1962 as Vice-Principal of Westcott House and then, from 1966, as Dean of Emmanuel. He has remained in Cambridge ever since, lecturing and writing about the philosophy of religion. He is the author of some 36 books. His broadcasting projects include 'The Sea of Faith' (BBC, 1984) which has grown into an international society.

Today, Don Cupitt's main activity is overseas. He is a Fellow of the Jesus Seminar, based at Santa Rosa, California, and his books appear from its publishing arm, the Polebridge Press. He is variously described as 'a radical theologian', 'a philosopher and experimental religious writer', 'a creative theologian', and 'an unsuccessful religious reformer'.

PETER J. GOMES is the Plummer Professor of Christian Morals and Preacher to Harvard University, USA. An ordained American Baptist minister, Gomes has been at Harvard since 1970. He holds 26 honorary degrees and is an honorary fellow of Emmanuel College, Cambridge.

His academic interests include biblical theology and criticism, hermeneutics, and ecclesiastical history. His major books, *The Good Book* and *The Good Life*, together with ten volumes of sermons and numerous articles, essays, and introductions, are generally concerned with Christian apologetics within the context of the modern secular university.

TREVOR HART is Professor of Divinity, Head of the School of Divinity and Principal of St Mary's College at the University of St Andrews. He is a priest in the Scottish Episcopal Church, and former Chair of the Doctrine Committee of that Church. He has written several books and numerous articles in systematic and historical theology. Among his most recent works are *Faith Thinking*, *Regarding Karl Barth* and *Hope Against Hope* (with Richard Bauckham). He is Director of the Institute for Theology, Imagination and the Arts at St Andrews, and is currently writing a two-volume 'poetics of redemption'.

ERIC JAMES was a friend of John Robinson for over 30 years, and was his literary executor and biographer. He was Canon Precentor of Southwark Cathedral during 1964–73, coinciding with John Robinson as Bishop of Woolwich. He is the author of numerous books, and for many years was a regular contributor to BBC Radio 4's *Thought for the Day*. He was Founder and Director of the charity Christian Action; is Chaplain to The Queen and was Select Preacher of Grays Inn, London.

ALISTER MCGRATH is Professor of Historical Theology, Oxford University, and Director of the Oxford Centre for Evangelism and Apologetics. He has published many best-selling works on theology, including the textbook *Christian Theology: An Introduction*, and has a particular interest in the interaction of faith and culture. Major recent books include *The Twilight of Atheism: The Rise and Fall of Disbelief in the Modern World* and *Dawkins' God: Genes, Memes and the Meaning of Life*.

MARTYN PERCY is Director of the Lincoln Theological Institute at the University of Manchester. He is also Adjunct Professor of Theology and Ministry at Hartford Seminary, Connecticut, USA. Since September 1999 he has served as a Council Member of the Advertising Standards Authority. He is also Canon Theologian of Sheffield Cathedral. His most recent book is *Salt of the Earth: Religious Resilience in a Secular Age* (T & T Clark International, 2002). Since 1999 he has been the Editor of *Modern Believing*. He is also a regular contributor to Radio 4, the BBC World Service, *The Independent*, *The Guardian* and other media.

CHRISTOPHER RYAN was Dean of King's College, Cambridge, the university which was so influential throughout John Robinson's life.

He studied for the priesthood at the Gregorian University in Rome and attended St Edmund's College, Cambridge, for postgraduate studies, later becoming Dean of the college. He was a scholar of medieval studies, with a special interest in the works of Dante, Aquinas and Michelangelo, and published significant research and commentary, among them his first widely respected book, *The Religious Roles of the Papacy 1150–1350*, a translation of Dante's *Convivio* and articles and books on the poetry of Michelangelo.

Christopher Ryan left the Roman Catholic Church in 1986 and was admitted to the Anglican Church. He married and began a fulfilling career as lecturer and then Professor of Italian at Sussex University.

In 2002 he was appointed Dean of King's College, Cambridge. He was the first priest since the Reformation to have been Dean of both a Roman Catholic college and an Anglican college in the same university.

Christopher Ryan died in February 2004 after a short illness.

COLIN SLEE is Dean of Southwark. After nearly two years as a VSO in Papua New Guinea, he trained at King's College, London, was ordained in 1970 and has worked in Norwich, Cambridge, St Albans and London. He was appointed to Southwark in 1994 and has contributed actively to the regeneration of the South Bank in the Bankside area, including major new buildings and restoration work at Southwark Cathedral. He has contributed to books on new religious movements and is a regular commentator on religious matters on television, radio and in the press.

JANE WILLIAMS was, until recently, tutor in doctrine at Trinity College, Bristol, and is now a freelance writer and lecturer. She contributed a regular column to *The Church Times* on the Sunday lectionary readings. These are now being published by SPCK as *Lectionary Reflections Year C* (2003), *Lectionary Reflections Year A* (2004). She has also written *Perfect Freedom* (Canterbury Press, 2001). When reading theology at Cambridge, she was taught New Testament theology by John Robinson.

Introduction

COLIN SLEE

During the summer of 2002 the Archdeacon of Southwark, the Venerable Douglas Bartles-Smith asked me what plans the Cathedral staff had to mark the fortieth anniversary of the publication of *Honest to God*. The brief answer was that we had no plans but were open to the idea of developing some if there was sufficient demand. The archdeacon suggested that I should discuss the idea with Canon Eric James, John Robinson's biographer, a relatively close neighbour and former Canon Missioner of Southwark Cathedral. As is always the case with Eric James, this conversation proved to be convivial, stimulating and fruitful. It left me with no illusions: there was clearly a demand for some sort of celebratory event, but what sort? The ultimate result was a training day for the clergy of the Diocese of Southwark in the form of a colloquium on *Honest to God* and its legacy, under the authority of the diocesan bishop, Tom Butler, held one day before the actual fortieth anniversary of the publication day, 21 March 1963. There were four pairs of lectures under the chairmanship of the Bishop of Kingston, Richard Cheetham. This book contains those lectures, each built around themes from the chapters of the book. What it cannot contain, however, is the other element of the occasion, something that is possibly more important than the lectures, I dare to suggest even possibly more important than the contents of *Honest to God* itself. The fortieth anniversary

supplied a glimpse into the nerve, energy and excitement of
theological and missiological enterprise in the 1960s. Being a
part of that enterprise was no less significant to those involved
than the mini-skirt, the Beatles, the introduction of the Morris
Mini and the flower-power era, which were also sweeping the
world in different strata of society at the same time.

It became very clear on the day of the colloquium that
people, and especially clergy from the Diocese of Southwark,
may be dated as 'Before Honest to God' (BHtG) and 'After
Honest to God' (AHtG). Those of us who are AHtG are at
a disadvantage when we try to appreciate the significance of
Robinson's slim volume. It is not simply a matter of theology. It was a watershed experience that changed lives, and
certainly the Church of England, far more than the relatively
few chapters themselves can represent. One of the lecturers
remarks that *Honest to God* was certainly not Robinson's
greatest theological work for the Church. In terms of scholarship and research, he made much weightier contributions in
New Testament studies. The importance of the book lay elsewhere.

Honest to God represents a phenomenon with several
facets. In the Diocese of Southwark it was, and to some extent
still remains, a symbol of the diocese's social engagement
and proclamation, and further, of its own self-awareness and
self-esteem, all of which developed considerably during that
period. It evokes for so many people emotional responses
indicating a total experience; it was much more than a book.
Whatever Mervyn Stockwood's gifts and weaknesses (and
there were many of each), his greatest gift to the Church at
large as Bishop of Southwark was that he created a diocese
filled with clergy willing to adventure in theology and in patterns of ministry. Witness the founding of the South London
Industrial Mission and the beginning of the Southwark Ordination Course, both initiatives that were later copied by the
Church in England and abroad. It was a period characterized

by debate, frequently fierce debate, which was seen as a necessary part of a common enterprise of evangelism and searching
after truth. The diocese still rejoices in a reputation for radicalism and honest speaking. That reputation is perhaps now too
self-conscious to be wholly justified or authentic, but it is the
fruit of the ecclesiastical volcano Mervyn gathered, a creative
force of energy that still has after-shocks.

On the fortieth anniversary of the publication of *Honest
to God*, many of us who are 'AHtG' saw people, some of
considerable age, gather from great distances to celebrate
a recognizable watershed. They are still energized by the
memory, the clergy capable of telling where they were when
the impact happened, rather as people can say where they
were when they heard of John F. Kennedy's assassination or
the death of Diana, Princess of Wales. Listening to their conversations was rather like being at a British Legion reunion,
hearing those 'What did you do during the War?' conversations among old comrades (and adversaries) in which no non-
participant can ever hope to share. The BHtGs who gathered
(many more who could not come sent messages from around
the world) may have been there as much to meet old friends as
to hear the lectures, but I hope they were pleased to discern the
book's continuing theological impact. I hope also that those
who were unable to be there will find this book a fitting com-
memoration and an enduring symbol of at least part of the
Honest to God legacy.

The *continuing* theological impact is crucial. We did not
want the colloquium or this book to be primarily retrospec-
tive or historical, but rather to be forward-looking. It would
have been impossible to recapture on one day in 2003 the
excitement and vigour of atmosphere and energy which bore
fruit in the months of 1963 and beyond, though we certainly
glimpsed some of it. But we saw that any attempt to replicate
it would be foolish and a failure. Our task is to move forward
in the adventure today.

Another aspect of the impact of *Honest to God* is shown in the publication figures for religious paperbacks. *Honest to God* went through three reprints in March 1963 alone. How many religious books experience that sort of immediate readership in their first month? It was translated in to 17 languages, ultimately selling over one million copies. It marked a sea change in paperback theology; possibly it *was* the sea change from hardback to paperback theological reading. That change is still reflected in bookshops and bookstalls at the west end of many churches, even on railway stations, where religious reading at reasonable prices is accessible. I well remember, when I was aged 17, my vicar encouraging the congregation of the west London church we attended to buy the book in order that he could run discussion groups and preach sermons denouncing it!

The first edition of *Honest To God* lists other SCM Press publications such as Michael Ramsey's invaluable *Introducing the Christian Faith*, but it was *Honest To God* that created an explosion of readership that was no longer restricted to clergy and theologians. Perhaps for the first time, too, it became generally realized that clergy are not necessarily theologians, nor vice versa. *Honest to God* not only blew away the rule book which defined the boundaries of theological adventuring, it also blew away the expectations of who might be considered the 'normal' theological reader, and marked an unmistakable watershed in theological debate within and beyond church membership.

Robinson remarks at the end of his short Preface: 'What I have tried to say, in a tentative and exploratory way, may seem to be radical, and doubtless to many heretical. The one thing of which I am fairly sure is that, in retrospect, it will be seen to have erred in not being nearly radical enough.'[1]

The present clergy chapter of Southwark Cathedral is composed of priests who are all 'AHtG'. We were anxious (perhaps also we were threatened) that any celebration of the publication of *Honest to God* should be much more than a nostalgic reunion of old warriors. We were very conscious that this book created mayhem when it was published. Many people demanded Robinson's resignation, and yet it rapidly became a standard text in theological colleges and university degree courses, and is now regarded as a very mild pussycat among significant radical texts. Robinson's prediction that 'it will be seen as having erred in not being nearly radical enough' has been fulfilled. We resolved, therefore, that two principles must mark the anniversary lectures: 1. They must be given by relatively young theologians, addressing the contribution *Honest to God* made to Christian thinking; looking forward rather than backward. 2. They must be drawn from a cross-section of the theological disciplines upon which Robinson touches, and from the whole cross-section of the Anglican tradition.

In the event, 'relatively young' became an elastic criterion. We were determined that Don Cupitt should be invited because we believed that some of his 'Sea of Faith' thinking emerged from a conviction of *Honest to God*'s being 'not nearly radical enough'; and that Colin Buchanan should be included because he personifies a contrasting perspective, and because he was, at the time, Bishop of Woolwich. Martyn Percy, Jane Williams and Trevor Hart can all be described as relatively young theologians. Christopher Ryan tragically died in 2004, but at the time of writing was 'young' at least in the Anglican Church, having previously been a Roman Catholic priest. Alister McGrath was invited as another leading representative of the conservative evangelical tradition in Anglican theology, and of a generation of evangelicals who would perhaps see themselves in conscious reaction to the tendency that *Honest to God* incarnates.

Our only non-Anglican, non-British invitee was the the Reverend Professor Peter J. Gomes, Plummer Professor of Christian Morals at Harvard and Pusey Minister in the Memorial Church of that university. John Harvard was born and baptized in Southwark; he left for the new world as part of the exodus of radical Puritan theologians who could not find a welcome within these shores, and he was benefactor to what is now the great university at Cambridge, Massachusetts that bears his name. The Southwark Cathedral staff and congregation value our links with that university very strongly. It was therefore a particular pleasure to invite Professor Gomes, an American Baptist who shares John Robinson's courage and zeal for saying the unsayable, proclaiming the truth revealed in the gospels with a new vocabulary for a contemporary context. In the event, however, Peter Gomes's contribution is limited to the covers of this book. The war in Iraq in 2003 started a few days before the colloquium, and he felt, rightly, that his place was with the staff and students of the university, of whom many would be directly affected by the conflict.

As Southwark's canon theologian, Jeffrey John took responsibility for the organization of the lectures with characteristic good humour and savoir-faire. In those early months of 2003 he was confidentially engaged in the process that in May culminated in his nomination by the Bishop of Oxford to become the next Bishop of Reading. This created a furore in the Anglican Communion and seized the interest of those 'outside' the Church in the same way as the furore surrounding the publication of *Honest to God*. There are further parallels. John Robinson was a bishop, Jeffrey John accepted nomination as a bishop. Jeffrey is a New Testament scholar and so was John Robinson – both of them relatively conservative in their own field, but both attacked for works written outside their main academic interest. *Honest to God*'s very title was about honesty, challenging the accepted boundaries of Anglican theological understanding. Jeffrey's 'offence' lay in his own honesty about his sexuality and his theological defence of faithful, covenanted same-sex relationships. Conservative hostility to John Robinson was increased by his defence of the publication of *Lady Chatterley's Lover*, which added a sexual frisson to the debate about his book. Conservative hostility to Jeffrey was plainly – and shamefully – fuelled solely by his homosexual orientation, since he is celibate, and his appointment was entirely within the rules and discipline of the Church of England. In both cases the Bishop of Southwark became involved in defending one of his senior staff against unprecedented attack. In both cases the Archbishop of Canterbury became embroiled in a controversy that suggested no satisfactory resolution. Both cases attracted enormous media interest (media coverage was overwhelmingly in support of Jeffrey John – rather less so in 1963 of John Robinson). In both cases the Church was divided in to 'camps' – the conservative evangelicals and conservative catholics on the one hand, and liberals and affirming catholics on the other.

Over 40 years however the background has changed. In 1963 a large corpus of the Church of England was 'middle of the road' or 'broad church'. This group has since been squeezed to the point at which in 2004 its very identity is in question, as the politicization of debate within the General Synod through groups such as Reform, Forward in Faith and the Movement for the Ordination of Women has developed. The irony, in the context of the lectures that constitute this book, is that the politicizing of debate sets up hard-edged boundaries of what is, or is not, acceptable as 'orthodoxy'; whereas Robinson was pleading for the dismantling of accepted boundaries precisely in order that new insights could be revealed by a God who transcends all boundaries. If Robinson's vision were to be truly realized, then the barriers between theological parties would dissolve, as all their perspectives would be seen as provisional, with no language, liturgy, biblical or doctrinal interpretation wholly sufficient in itself.

Honest to God was published as regular attendance at church was beginning a steep decline (a membership decline that affected other institutions – for example, political parties and trades unions – equally sharply). Robinson recognized that one inevitable response would be increased introversion in the Church – a refusal to engage with contemporary culture, and a call simply to preach the traditional doctrines of the Church in the same way and in the same language even more loudly and aggressively. Seeing the dangers of this move to retrenchment, he pleaded that the Church of England should remain theologically and socially an inclusive church. The hounding and condemnation of Jeffrey John during the summer of 2003 demonstrated Robinson's foresight and the fulfilment of his worst fears.

On the fortieth anniversary of the publication of *Honest to God*, it is noteworthy that the National Census figures show that 73 per cent of the adult population describe themselves as Christian, 52 per cent as Anglican. Some 30 per cent of the population claim to go to church regularly (all denominations); the Church of England's own figures indicate 15 per cent entering its doors with some regularity. Among Anglicans alone, therefore, the question must be asked: 'What has driven away the 37 per cent of the population who describe themselves as Anglican yet never attend church?' They far outnumber those Anglicans who attend. There is within these figures, an important message for the Church. It is at least possible (I would argue it is probable) that strident, partisan, doctrinaire and frequently self-righteous churchmanship has contributed most to alienating and excluding the very people whom Robinson was seeking to reach and include: the seekers after truth, the ones who need a mature faith capable of a wide variation of expression; those who are open to new insights and new revelation in knowledge and experience; those who understand that tradition and doctrine have always been changing and developing, and must do so to live. We need to look very carefully at what we mean by evangelism and what we do to further it. The current understanding and approach may well be achieving the opposite of its stated aim – as the results of the much-vaunted 'Decade of Evangelism' seem to testify.

In his masterly biography of Archbishop Michael Ramsey, Professor Owen Chadwick records Ramsey's response to *Honest to God* and the ensuing imbroglio. Ramsey, Chadwick says, later regretted the severity of his judgement at the time:

> A decade later, when he looked back upon the controversy, he thought that his reaction was mistaken. He confessed to Mervyn Stockwood, who blamed him for being unduly harsh, that his reaction had indeed been over-harsh and unsympathetic. A reader of the documents after Ramsey's death will find this absurd self-deprecation. He continued to think that the author of *Honest to God* was not profound enough in what he then wrote and that some of his expressions were negative without necessity. But always afterwards he saw Robinson's mind for the Christian mind that it was. Always later he regretted that the doubtful reputation that Robinson gained from *Lady Chatterley's Lover* and these events prevented him from receiving the place in the Church which was his due.
>
> On reflection, Ramsey realized that the hullabaloo was symptomatic of a crisis of faith in the nation, and that it needed treatment different from that of his first reaction. It showed gropings, conscious and unconscious, among many people on the periphery of faith. It needed more understanding than contradiction.[2]

With the luxury of 40 years' hindsight, it is possible to see in *Honest to God* a bishop publishing in accessible language, at an accessible price, what theologians and many others beyond the regular membership of the Church had been saying for some while. Robinson's offence, therefore, was honesty in advance of the institution's capacity to cope with it. This offence was compounded by his position as a bishop. Bishops still make much of their role as a focus of unity within the Church, and are sometimes taken unawares when they find it

comes into conflict with their role as shepherds who must lead
the flock to pastures new. Robinson's work could not be dismissed as the abstract and irrelevant musings of an academic
theologian precisely because he was a bishop. This poses the
question whether we have realistic expectations of our bishops,
and in particular, whether we really want them to be theologians. This is an issue about episcopacy that the Church has
not progressed in 40 years, as was evident when David Jenkins
became Bishop of Durham. The idea that a bishop can be a
focus for unity *through* stimulating and leading his flock in
theological debate seems to be one that has not yet surfaced
within the House of Bishops.

Michael Ramsey's regrets about his treatment of John
Robinson and the loss of his episcopal ministry make timely
and salutary reading. I have little doubt that the Church of
England will look back on the 'Jeffrey John affair' of 2003
– perhaps on the fortieth anniversary of his honesty with God
and the Church – and marvel at the Church's rejection of a
truthful, celibate, homosexual bishop. It may be that in a
future biography of Rowan Williams, he too will be recorded
as concluding that his decisions in 2003 were unnecessarily
severe and had prevented another good man from receiving
the place in the Church which was his due.

The contemporary relevance of *Honest to God*, and of
the forward perspective we gave it in the colloquium on its
fortieth anniversary, thus became sadly clear in the months
immediately following. The Christian Church seeks to be the
guardian of truth as revealed in Holy Scripture. She is therefore always reluctant to accommodate change, and demands
a very heavy price from those who seek to proclaim the gospel
afresh. These eight lecturers acknowledge that *Honest to God*
was not a great theological book, and certainly not Robinson's *magnum opus,* but that it was nevertheless a seminal
book through what it achieved. They differ in their estimate
of the book's own worth, and in their assessment of its impor-

tance for their own area of theology. What they all agree on
(and this is of such enormous importance that it is amazing
how easily it is overlooked in all the storms of 40 years and
more) is that the central tasks of understanding and reinter-
preting scripture, of speaking about God in an intelligible way
to our own culture, of finding an authentic Christian ethic for
the conditions of life today, are all as important in 2003 as
in 1963, and that the language of 1963 will no longer serve.
Robinson's legacy is therefore very healthy. The lecturers are
not agreed about how that legacy should be pursued, but they
might agree that their very lack of agreement is itself a positive
result of that legacy: grist to the mill, part of the way forward
– because it helps us all to test and mature our faith as we try
to be Honest to God.

Colin Slee
Rhoscolyn, Anglesey
New Year's Day 2004

NOTES

1 J. A. T. Robinson, *Honest to God*, SCM Press, 1963, p. 10.
2 Owen Chadwick, *Michael Ramsey, A Life*, Clarendon Press, 1990,
   p. 370ff.

1. Honest to God: In Its Time and Since

COLIN BUCHANAN

I have two minor claims – thoughtfully conceded by today's management – to give this opening paper.[1] The first is that I am myself Bishop of Woolwich, fourth after John Robinson in a colourful line of succession. I am in my seventh year as such and am honestly very used to the role, and very used to the Bishop of Woolwich being me. So I have an odd and disturbing feeling when, as in the last few days, I find myself again surrounded by all the literature (including the journalism) of the 1960s and read in it of controversy raised by 'the Bishop of Woolwich'. And as he is appraised, praised, and also vilified, so I say resolutely to myself 'no, not you – it was that other fellow 40 years ago'. In fact, whatever my own vibes, few of my contemporaries have ever confused me with John Robinson.[2]

My other claim is that, alone among today's contributors, my pastoral ministry covered both then and now. I was already ordained when *Honest to God* was published; I had to respond to it pastorally. I preached on it once – some months late.[3] To my grief, I have lost the text of my sermon, but its thrust was to warn of the futility of taking the Bishop of Woolwich too seriously.[4] At the time the main issue that had struck us was the famous *Observer* headline on the Sunday two days before publication 'Our Image of God must go'.[5] This preceded – and duly multiplied – the sales of the book on the Tuesday. The *Observer* headline not only caught people's attention; it also stirred memories. People recalled that this Bishop had given evidence on behalf of the unexpurgated *Lady Chatterley's Lover* three years before – he was dangerous, and engaged in brinkmanship. Puritan though our congregation might be, the doctrine of God was probably of more concern to them than the dangers of the unleashed libido. At any rate, to me, as one up to his ears in parochial ministry, *Honest to God* was no mere subject in the doctrine paper of my General Ordination Exam – I was ministering to some hundreds of adults and teenagers when the book came out, and recognized some need to guide them.

So did it reshape my theology? Was I liberated like a butterfly out of a chrysalis, as occasionally people seem to say? My answer is drawn from a poet you will know:

Myself when young did cautiously frequent
the Bishop of Woolwich, and heard much argument
about it and about; yet evermore
came out the same door wherein I went.[6]

So let us start with the image. It is central in the *Observer* article, almost equally so in *Honest to God* itself, and seen as such by the various critics – I have a clutch to hand, and a further plethora in David Edwards's own collection of responses.[7]

The old image is of God as 'up there'. Robinson writes as though this was an accidental or arbitrary choice of language and thought, an unhelpful image which 'must go'. It is associated in his mind with the triple-decker universe of the heavens, the earth, and some place beneath the earth, which he believes was the universal thought-frame from Abraham to Copernicus. It belongs with an age of childhood in the human race. We still have it, of course, in popular language, but Robinson would reckon it was an outmoded and unhelpful survival. Now I think there is another side to that argument, and I think it worth taking time on.

Admittedly, we are more used to speaking of the 'sky' when we mean the blue dome 'above' our heads, and of 'heaven' when we mean the abode of God, or of the blessed. But the persistence of biblical language has us saying 'when I behold the heavens, the works of your fingers', as we also refer to the planets as 'heavenly bodies'.[8] Unbelief has always enjoyed thinking that Christians believe in heaven as a place with specific co-ordinates within the created universe, where there is a 'home for little children above the bright blue sky'. That cartoon reached its denouement in 1960, when Gagarin, the first human into space, came back and reported, really as concluding the argument, that he had not seen God up there. But, as so often in controversies about God, he was denying what believers were not asserting.

But upness and downness are *not* mere accretions to our understanding of God. They are built into our very nature as earthlings. Let me illustrate by a rapid cumulation of examples, a cumulation which I hope you will find forceful.

Genesis says the Spirit of God hovered 'over' the face of the waters. From then on power and control belong to those who are above; and conformity and obeisance belong to those below. When God forms man (and woman) from the dust of the earth, you subliminally take aboard that he is 'above' his creation, working it as we might create a crib scene or an Easter garden. Actually the surprise comes when God simply 'walks in the garden'; but it is that which is the unexpected imagery, and the norm is much more that God is looking 'down' on the garden, on its map, its contents, its inhabitants – and he knows it all *because* he is above it. You can see things from above, and you can see things in an entirety, which you never can if you live on the surface, behind the trees, and think you can escape notice. Furthermore, in those early chapters, God is the God who sends the sun, sets his rainbow in the clouds, and is clearly 'over' all earthly activity.

They started a tower of Babel – a tower to bring them 'up' to heaven – God 'came down' to see them. God promised the birth of Isaac, he then 'went up' from Abraham (Gen. 17.24). In the next chapter God says he will 'go down' to Sodom and Gomorrah and inspect them. Abraham goes to slaughter Isaac, the angel calls to him 'from heaven'. Jacob has a dream at Bethel, the ladder reaches 'up' from earth to heaven; the Lord stands 'above' it. The children of Israel suffer in Egypt; God 'looks down' on them and 'comes down' to deliver them.

There are, no doubt, other models of divinities – but they are animistic and pantheistic ones. I suggest to you that all models of an omnipotent God who is other than we are are conveyed to us by 'upness'. And so it is in all the Old Testament – we expect to 'exalt' God and to 'humble' ourselves and be 'lowly' (you will recognize 'exalt' means 'lift up', and that 'humble ourselves' means to 'go to ground' [Latin, *humus* – 'ground'] – and so too to 'humiliate' ourselves). Elijah is 'taken up' into heaven; Naaman 'bows down in the house of Rimmon'; God says in Isaiah 'To me every knee shall bow' – Paul applies that to Jesus.

So we have in our creed, rooted in the New Testament, of Jesus, that 'For us and for our salvation he *came down* from heaven . . . he *ascended* into heaven'. For myself, I believe the description of Jesus physically ascending – yes, going up – into the clouds at his ascension. This again is not to locate him as physically just 'up there' – a yard or two only just out of sight. But it is both to say that 'upness' is integral to Godheadness, and, as a contingent fact, that the disciples needed total assurance that his appearances on earth had finished and they were now to live not by sight but by faith. The actual transition of Jesus obviously did happen a little out of our sight; but what came to our sight was the Lord going 'up'. So Stephen looks up into heaven (or sky!), and sees Jesus standing at the right hand of God.[9] Sacrifices too are offered 'up'.

The 'upness' is not unique to God. It is shot through our earthly thought-structures – people go 'up' in the world, 'up' in other people's estimation, 'up' in class, 'up' in rank, 'up' in responsibility. They feel small, or got down, put down, humiliated by other people's treatment. They ride 'high', go 'to the top' (or 'over the top'), and they are put 'over' other people. When that happens, we then look 'up' to them. They are 'superior' or 'inferior'. In one sense it is all metaphor – but so integral to life that we cannot unthink it, and yet it is a metaphor so transparent that we easily distinguish between going up a class at school, while physically descending to a classroom one floor lower.

So, to return to God, it is in liturgy, springing from the Bible, that 'upness' flowers. We can hardly stop saying 'Glory to God in the highest', 'Lift up your hearts', 'Raise thou me heavenward'. Kneeling and prostrating, bowing and genuflecting, looking down in humility and up in adoration, even raising your arms in praise – all these are three-dimensional quasi-sacramental outworkings of the language of God being 'up'. And the hymnody is pretty fierce, not only in the children's verse involving '. . . above the bright blue sky.' For we find ourselves as adults also singing: 'Now above the sky he's king . . .' and I suspect that verb to 'soar' has the same implications ('Soar we now where Christ has led' and 'Till I soar through tracts unknown . . .').

Now Robinson thinks that we take all this literally and, by so doing, fix our minds into triple-decker-universe mould – which is perhaps the infantile stage of humanity. But, if only we would, we could gain from Tillich a metaphor in 'ground of our being', and, if we did that, we would with some maturity know that that is a metaphor – which we were failing to do with the old image of 'upness'. I think that is where the heart of his argument lies. But I submit that dispensing with the 'up' is not so much wrong as virtually impossible. 'The ground of our being' was a metaphor that 'rang bells' (another metaphor of the sixties) for Robinson.[10] Everywhere here and there you can still find people for whom it 'rang bells'. But it does very little to illuminate most of us, as it can only be inserted into our thinking by a wholesale attack upon the existing grain of our thinking and our subconsciousnesses. To most of us, it is not a deliverance but a threatened brainwash.

A threat does lie there, for the change, if made, is actually dangerous and undesirable. For 'ground of our being', even if it rings bells, does actual harm. For the 'upness' and 'above-ness' of God are not only the most regular metaphors which come to hand; they are also the guarantees of God's 'other-ness'. They convey to us his standing as our creator. They give us starting points for a personal relationship. We relate to God because we begin with two distinguishable entities with distance between them – God and us. Upness and downness ensure that the relationship is understood as an asymmetrical one – the down are not exactly peers with the up. Of course the fierce distant monotheism which that might imply is wholly altered by God's presence with us, both in the incarnation and atonement, and in the Holy Spirit's presence with us, and the whole consequent doctrine that we are the temple of God, the 'place' of his dwelling by the Spirit. Whatever approaches to orthodoxy Robinson makes with his Christology, there opens a credibility gap if Jesus is presenting himself to his disciples with the ticket 'whoever has seen me has seen the ground of his [or her] being'. All issues of an accountable relationship with a God who is other – yes, and a God who provides a mediator – start to collapse. Alan Richardson said of Tillich's thesis 'One cannot pick a quarrel with the ground of one's being, but, then, one cannot go to the stake for it either.'[11] And Alan Richardson's presupposition is clearly a God who is 'other' than we are – and that is basic to Christian theism.

A reflection from 40 years on – a mildly put critique in itself, but one which is nevertheless in effect a dismissive obituary – came from Stephen Sykes in last Friday's *Church Times*, 'John Robinson knew well enough that such language was metaphorical, and that "down under" was no less a metaphor than "up there". He seems to have underestimated the sophistication that enables religious people to effect the translation in their heads.'[12]

When Robinson has done his stuff with Tillich's phrase, he then lays Bonhoeffer under contribution. Man has now 'come of age' – he does not now need 'religion'. It looks as though Bonhoeffer meant that discipleship (which he surely always viewed as a costly surrender?) should no longer consist in looking for God to forgive and overcome our weaknesses, with an ultimately self-centred agenda. David Jenkins writes 'This would seem to be a splendid and justified protest against the so-largely prevalent religious policy and practice which turns God into a cosmic anodyne and makes religion the enemy, not the crown, of life.'[13] But if this is what Bonhoeffer meant by our 'coming of age' and being 'religionless' – which is a very particular meaning to give it – what did Robinson mean? His long quotation from Bonhoeffer seems to be a denunciation of a 'God of the gaps' apologetic.[14] Robinson seems to be saying he is quoting this in order to clear the decks for a replacing theology. Certainly, there was a vogue in the 1960s for speaking of an enlightened and enlightening 'religionless' Christianity. It led in the late 1960s, I think, to theologians interested in the death of God.[15] But all such language is multivocal, and anyone using it has a great duty to spell out univocally just the sense in which it is used. Certainly, I am unclear what replacing theology Robinson is setting before us. The puzzle is heightened where, further on, he has a footnote in which he gives a definition of Tillich's of 'religion': 'Religion is not a special function of man's spiritual life, but it is the dimension of depth in all of its functions.'[16] Now we need a definition if we are to gain the key to being 'religionless' – though in fact I am not greatly helped by this one. But then Robinson, having said, 'Ultimately I believe Tillich is right', goes on, infuriatingly, to add 'I have preferred to retain the customary usage in order to bring out the point of Bonhoeffer's critique'; and we are left wholly unclear as to what the 'customary usage' can be. Indeed I retain a funny suspicion that, if I asked all present today what the defining characteristics of 'religionless Christianity' might be, many would have perfectly clear ideas about it – but, on inspection, the various ideas thus produced would cancel each other out, and corporate unclarity would return. The same effect, of purporting to show us a bright light and then leading us into semi-darkness, recurs with the 'coming of age' metaphor. It is used boldly in *Honest to God*, and the reader gets some sense of the relative responsibility modern man must carry for himself, without props or nannying. But something has happened to it, and coming of age is cut, in a footnote in *The Honest to God Debate,* to 'I should be perfectly prepared to accept in its place the notion that man has reached adolescence.'[17] Now I ask you – he has quickly traded in the achieved maturity, and left us instead with humanity at an age of recognizable irresponsibility.[18]

Now I do want to pay tribute to John Robinson as a biblical scholar. He has perhaps not had much notice as a member of the New Testament panel of the New English Bible.[19] He has had considerable applause for *The Body,* for his *Twelve New Testament Studies*; most of us would be intrigued by *The Priority of John*; all of us ought to wrestle with *Redating the New Testament*; I hope one day to engage with *The Human Face of God.*[20] But has he the stature as an apologist or a dogmatic theologian that the sales of *Honest to God* suggest? I observe that in David Jenkins's book *Guide to the Debate about God* (1966) Robinson does not qualify for a chapter. If that is the view of a discerning (and not unsympathetic) theologian just three years after publication of *Honest to God*, how do we account for those enormous waves made initially and the rare mini-ripples still surviving only a short time after? And I fear it is arguable that the extraordinary sales of *Honest to God* are attributable to non-theological factors, rather than a widespread breakthrough about the doctrine of God. The interest resulted from a combination of initial boosts, which I shall spell out, and then to the commercially successful spiral deriving from the very publicity of high initial sales. So I put it to you that there was built in to the initial sales an element of what might well be called luck.

The luck lies in three antecedent features, a catchy title and a contextual factor.

First there was *Lady Chatterley*. Robinson's testimony less than three years before on behalf of D. H. Lawrence's most sexually explicit book gave him a national profile as a slightly risqué character.

Second, he was, of course, a bishop, and a bishop from whom, as it seemed, the Archbishop of Canterbury was feeling some need to protect us.[21] I have never much expected myself that a suffragan bishop has widespread power to shock or intrigue, but Eric James in his splendid biography makes quite a bit of this, and I think, as I recall the time myself, that that is true.[22]

Third, the *Observer* article with its flaming headlines 'Our Image of God must go' caught the imagination – and not just the imagination of the faithful, I suspect, but also the curiosity of the doubting, the lapsing, the broad-minded intellectuals, even the opponents, possibly the enquirer. The sell-out on the first day must be due in large part to that headline.

Along with those factors was the title. John Bowden wrote in the thirtieth anniversary symposium: 'I know of only one other recent title that has proved to have quite the power, for better or worse, as *Honest to God,* and that is Salman Rushdie's *The Satanic Verses*. In each case the title has gone on to lead a life of its own . . .'[23] There is reason to think that the title owed quite a bit to Ruth Robinson.

I suspect there a final further factor – nothing else competed in the news with *Honest to God*. It was not the Profumo week – and it would have been different if it had been. Compare the death of C. S. Lewis, later that year; then a great apologist gained hardly an obituary. Why not? Simple – because he died within a few hours of Kennedy being shot. Now apart from politics there was plenty religiously in the 1960s to grab headlines – Vatican II on a world scene (the First Session was just over, and John XXIII died soon after), various initiatives on the Southwark scene – and I commend James Bogle's book, *South Bank Religion*[24] – the charismatic movement (datable to 1962), the Keele Congress (April 1967), even the start of liturgical experiment (which I was in on in 1966–8) – but, I submit, little else to swamp newspaper headlines in Robinson's week. Bear in mind, too, that heterodoxy is more newsworthy in the secular world than orthodoxy. He scooped the pool.

But here I am in south-east London 40 years later. Has John Robinson led to a revival of dynamic Christianity? Yes, life was colourful with Mervyn as bishop. Yes, Parish and People and *Prism* pamphlets viewed themselves as the cutting edge of renewal of liturgy; then the Southwark Ordination Course and South London Industrial Mission, a rethinking of morality, *Honest to God* and John Robinson's further works, a great ferment of ideas on the South Bank, all these gave some a sense of being in at the birth of a new theological age, an unprecedented renaissance. *Honest to God* is reported as having unbelievers talking religion in pubs, in the way that David Jenkins's later denials of the resurrection is supposed to have done. But still I ask whether the Robinson book ways of talking about God are plausible, are marketable (in other words, whether they are truly missionary), are powerful (whether they transform lives) and whether they have been successful.

I am a strong believer in frontier work. One de facto attraction of the Church of England is that the worker on the frontier is unlikely to be tried for heresy. But the evidence of history is that Robinsonianism had little mileage in it. The decline in the number of ordinands of the Church of England began around the time of *Honest to God*, and particularly in the parts of the Church most likely to follow him. Liturgical revision emerged in the next three years without reference to new images of God (not because of ignorance – we had the South Bank strong on the Commission – but because it will not go into liturgy). Clearly the liturgy and the conservatism of its forms, including hymnody, has deeply affected faith and spirituality. (In passing, Robinson mentions in *But That I Can't Believe* that he has found little in the way of liturgy that expresses his theology; but he mentions a service in 1967 written by some young people in Edgware entitled 'Be Yourself'.[25]) The breaking of the barrier between sacred and secular, in so far as it has been achieved, owes little to his spadework. The modern evangelical resurgence – and its galloping offspring the charismatic movement – ignored Robinson. Our brothers and sisters in African and other provinces have expanded and grown on wholly traditional language of worship and evangelism. The evangelists and apologists in England of the last four decades have proved to be far more biblically conservative also – I mention Lesslie Newbigin, Alister McGrath (with us today), Tom Wright, Michael Nazir-Ali, Stephen Sykes, David Ford. The shaping of the Church of today, of its leaders and of its people, owes little or nothing to John Robinson's theology of his South Bank days. Of course we need frontier people; of course they may try to change the frontiers a little. But they only have their task because there is a core gospel with frontiers to it and exponents of it. They are in the last analysis sucker shoots – they only have life because the traditional gospel gave them a place of departure from which to grow. And it abides when they have gone. So you see how I came out the same door as in I went.

NOTES

1 The original title given to both my paper and Martyn Percy's to open the day's symposium on 20 March was 'Culture and Context: *Honest to God*'s attempt to relate doctrine to contemporary thought and the situation today'. I have edited both title and contents for publication (including the allocating of side thoughts or explanations to footnotes), but hope it still reads as though delivered live.

2 I write this without value judgements. I go on lower down to express appreciation of his theologizing in Cambridge before and after being Bishop of Woolwich. But I found on 20 March that Eric James, the biographer of J. A. T. R., who was present for the seminar, was grieved that no tribute had been paid to John Robinson for his pastoral ministry. I think this is true, but it was built into the brief to which the speakers conformed. For the seminar day was not entitled 'John Robinson' but '*Honest to God*', and we largely confined ourselves to that topic. But I know there are many to speak gratefully of the leadership and pastoral care John Robinson gave in south-east London in his time.

3 It was late for two reasons: firstly, one had to wait to see if the interest would last long enough for it to be worth confronting (though there may have been asides in earlier sermons); but, secondly, my copy of *Honest to God* is a fourth printing – I could not respond on the spot, for you could not get copies in a Manchester suburb. The printings are indistinguishable, save that the first printing – the Penny Black edition – had the photo of J. A. T. R. on the back cover in an exotic shirt and sports jacket and tie and an uncomfortable laugh, and these apparently sold out on 19 March, the day of publication. In subsequent printings he reverted to dog-collar and pectoral cross and a donnish self-composure.

4 Possibly contemporary curates give the same warning about the contemporary Bishop of Woolwich.

5 It is always called a 'headline' – it was actually the headline to the *Observer*'s 'Weekend Review', a supplement tucked into the main paper.

6 Paraphrased from Edward Fitzgerald, *The Rubáiyát of Omar Khayyám*, Quatian 27.

7 These are: A. M. Ramsey, *Image Old and New*, SPCK, 1963; A Richardson (ed.), *Four Anchors from the Stern*, SCM, 1963; J. I. Packer, *Keep Yourselves from Idols*, Church Book Room Press, 1963; O. Fielding Clarke, *For Christ's Sake*, REP, 1963; D. Edwards (ed.); *The Honest to God Debate*, SCM, 1963; and Leon Morris, *The Abolition of Religion*, IVF, 1964.

8 The somewhat joking reverse metaphor refers to clergy as 'sky-pilots'.

9 Even the pagan Lycaonians said of Paul and Barnabas 'The Gods have come "down" to us in human likeness' (Acts 14.11).

10 It looks as though he bought up some paragraphs of Tillich almost verbatim. The heart of it all lies here: 'ground of all being . . . For if you know that God means depth, you know much about Him . . . he who knows about depth knows about God' – Tillich, *The Shaking of the Foundations*, Pelican, 1949, pp. 62–3; J. I. Packer handles this most brutally: '. . . its ideas are surprisingly secondhand; it is just a plateful of mashed-up Tillich fried in Bultmann and garnished with Bonhoeffer' (*Keep Yourselves from Idols*, p. 5).

11 *Four Anchors from the Stern*, p. 6.

12 Stephen Sykes in *Church Times*, 14 March 2003.

13 David Jenkins, *Guide to the Debate about God*, Lutterworth, 1966, p. 102.

14 Robinson, *Honest to God*, pp. 36–7.

15 The 'death of God' theological fashion, associated with Thomas Altizer, is difficult to recapture today, perhaps because it did not capture most of us in the first place. But it is worth investigation as to how far the (already existing) concepts that Robinson deployed – image changed to 'ground of our being', man 'come of age', and 'religionless Christianity' – were the upstream pollutants that led downstream to 'the death of God'.

16 Robinson, *Honest to God*, p. 86, note 2.

17 The full note reads: 'This phrase has been endlessly misunderstood, despite my footnote on p. 104. I should be perfectly prepared to accept in its place the notion that man has reached adolescence' (Edwards, *The Honest to God Debate*, p. 270, note 3). The note in *Honest to God* to which he refers would in my judgement assist the process of misunderstanding 'come of age', rather than clarify its meaning.

18 The aforesaid note is actually disavowing any overtones of maturity in the phrase 'come of age' which might therefore exculpate him from any implication of immaturity in the use of 'adolescence'. But that would be by special exclusion from the term one of the most natural meanings of it. And, typically of Robinson, he does not attempt to qualify or limit the meaning of the word 'adolescence' which he has just tossed into the argument.

19 Eric James gives some space to this – including a photograph – in his biography.

20 Perhaps this array of titles justifies my general contention that I far prefer what my predecessor as Bishop of Woolwich wrote when in

Cambridge (before and after his South Bank days) to anything that he produced *as* Bishop of Woolwich.

21 It agitated Mervyn Stockwood, his diocesan, also. He was in correspondence with Michael Ramsey, urging him of the problem it would cause if the Bishop of Woolwich were classified as a heretic by the Archbishop of Canterbury. Michael Ramsey had three separate cracks at *Honest to God*: one in a TV programme, one in his pamphlet *Image Old and New*, and one in his presidential address to the Canterbury Convocation in May 1963. But he was skilled in raising questions about what message the book would convey, rather than whether the author was orthodox or heterodox.

22 People with shorter memories will recall the shock when David Jenkins, nominated as Bishop of Durham, virtually denied the resurrection of Christ at Easter 1984. But David Jenkins himself thought he was only engaging publicly in the kind of reflection (or speculation) that had marked his days as Professor of Theology at Leeds. He discovered that a bishop really is supposed to articulate the historic faith in a reasonably accessible form, and bishops who do not – as in 1963 it had seemed John Robinson did not – are the subjects of scandalized attack, because of their official teaching office in the Church.

23 John Bowden, 'Concerning Theism' in John Bowden (ed.), *Thirty Years of Honesty*, SCM Press, 1993, p. 20.

24 This has just been published by the author's own initiative: James Bogle, *South Bank Religion: The Diocese of Southwark 1959–1969*, Hatcham Press, 2003. It is a splendid first glance for outsiders at that which South Bankers have known well for 40 years.

25 *But That I Can't Believe*, Collins, 1967, p. 117 – He could hardly know that I was myself the guest preacher at that service, and that I somewhat unsympathetically took as my text Jesus saying, 'Let a man deny himself'; but then the people who planned the service and submitted it to him were not the normal youth group, but a bunch of powerfully led entryists.

2. A Lasting Legacy?

MARTYN PERCY

Where were you in 1963? Most people who are old enough can recall something of that year. It was the year John F. Kennedy was shot. The Cuban missile crisis had been and gone. The Beatles had already had a few number one hits, but 'Beatle-mania' was yet to be. The world of fashion was turning, and the world of politics in some turmoil. We'd never had it so good, the night of the long knives, the publication of *Lady Chatterley's Lover* and the 'Profumo Affair'; the '1960s' – a decade of revolution, experimentation and change – was now well underway. And John Robinson's *Honest to God* – a curious little paperback from SCM publishers – was part of that cultural sea change.

Arguably, were it not for the abstract and interview printed in *The Observer* the previous Sunday and the fact that the author was a bishop in the Church of England, we probably never would have heard of this book. But as is so often the case, events, time and context play their part in lifting an accessible, intriguing and influential monograph into the category of the famous, if not notorious. Reading *Honest to God* today, one could honestly ask, 'what is all the fuss about?' The piece seems pretty tame and many of its central tenets are things that many people would take for granted. So arguably, we remember *Honest to God*, not so much for what it said, as for the effect it had and the residual resonance that continues to ripple through the Church. To understand the impact of *Honest to God*, one has to understand something of the cultural context of Britain in the 1960s.

Earlier in the year, an influential book, and to my mind a much more interesting, deeper piece of work – had been published. Alec Vidler's edited collection of essays, *Soundings: Essays Concerning Christian Understanding*, had set an anticipatory and mildly radical tone for 'new' thinking in Anglicanism, in the wake of the burgeoning prosperity of the post-war years. *Soundings* took its title from a quote attributed to Miles Smith, Bishop of Gloucester from 1612 to 1624: 'Man hath but a shallow sound and a short reach and dealeth only by probabilities and likelihoods.'

The book's cautionary, temperate tone in relation to doctrine, authority and the historicity of Scripture, was typical of several publications that marked a sea change in the way in which theology was regarded within the academy and more generally in the public sphere – not least within the Church itself. *Soundings* contained essays from John Habgood, George Wood, Harry Williams, Ninian Smart, Joseph Sanders, Hugh Montefiore, Geoffrey Lampe and Alec Vidler himself. The essays are thoughtful and prescient, and could almost be said to be teasingly probing in their orientation.

But this is only the world of theology. More generally in society, the early 1960s marked a range of significant changes, of which *Honest to God* can be said to be a product as well as a cause. Iconoclasm was in. Alternatives to the mainstream were also in. Questioning and questing was in; journeys, pilgrimages, new epiphanies of knowledge, and experimentation with alternative lifestyles were beginning to take off. Furthermore, radicalism had a point to it. Authority was no longer taken for granted. In order to prove its worth and to keep its place, it had to argue, and not assert.

It was into this cultural milieu that *Honest to God* emerged. Tentatively we might say that *Honest to God* questioned the right of authority to assert itself; answers now had to be *argued* for. Moreover, judging by the reaction of many readers to the book, it would appear that one of the legacies of *Honest to God* was that it liberated people from the hard husk of traditionalism and certainty, and gave them the kernel of faith, which of course necessarily made space for doubt. In other words, it freed people to think about and doubt the church, which is itself essential for a mature faith and a developing church. Unquestionably, *Honest to God* also brought theology into the public sphere and took it out of control of the Church, arguably to its great advantage. In short, it made people think, and invited them to reason.

It may also be true to say that *Honest to God* did not damage the Church per se. The theological timbre of the book is remarkably temperate, even a little self-effacing. It is really the inability of the church to cope with the critical acclaim and interest that *Honest to God* generated that proved to be problematic. As John Lawrence notes from his book review from the summer of 1963:

> A little book can make a great stir. *Honest to God* has brought to a wide public some ideas which, in one form or another, have long been discussed among theologians both lay and clerical; and in his chapter on prayer Dr Robinson makes an important contribution to the debate. Whatever one may think of the bishop's tentative conclusions – and it's only fair to emphasise that his conclusions are tentative – it is good to have these questions brought to the surface.[1]

Similarly, C. S. Lewis, then Professor of Medieval and Renaissance English at Cambridge University, in his review in *The Observer* on 24 March, comments that:

> The Bishop of Woolwich will disturb most of us Christian laymen less than he anticipates. We have long abandoned

belief in a God who sits on a throne in a localised heaven. We call that belief anthropomorphism and it was officially condemned before our time. There is something about this in Gibbon. I have never met any adult who replaced 'God up there' by 'God out there' in the sense 'spatially external to the universe'.[2]

Later in his review, Lewis concedes that:

his view of Jesus as a window seems wholly orthodox – 'he that hath seen me hath seen the Father'. So perhaps the real novelty is in the Bishop's doctrine about God. But we can't be certain, for here he is very obscure. He draws a sharp distinction between asking, "Does God exist as a person?" and asking whether ultimate reality is personal. But surely he who says yes to the second question has said yes to the first.[3]

Elsewhere, the public were more divided. One of the greater achievements of *Honest to God* is the enormous postbag that it generated, as well as the sheer volume of sales for its publisher, SCM Press. Thus, typical letters in the favourable camp include the following quotes:

This is *just* the kind of thing which we have needed, in this University certainly, and I believe elsewhere in this country, to stir up the discussion, not only with Christians, but also among self-styled atheists and agnostics. Many people in this University who have seen the book are deeply grateful to you for this courageous piece of writing.[4]

For many, reading this has been a conversion experience, with all the emotional clarity and mental confusion that they have ridiculed in fundamentalists since they clambered maturely out of the pram.[5]

With all my heart I know you are right, and that somehow
Christ is struggling free from the grave clothes of our
binding, and that a revolution, or resurrection, of Christian
thinking is most marvellously in the making.[6]

I agree that this is a tremendously exciting time to be alive in
the history of the Church – though we may well be coming
to a sort of end to the history of the Church. This is a revolution of far greater consequence than Luther's and Calvin's,
of the same order of consequence as Constantine's.[7]

Others were less enthused:

Of your own contribution in *Honest to God*, I fear I am
somewhat critical. I lunched with [a friend] – when I was
in London recently – and we spent most of the time talking
about your book and article. We both agreed that *Honest
to God* was 'woolly', not likely to convince the intelligent,
while the simple would not know what it was all about,
except that it seemed to be taking their God away from
them.[8]

I want you to know that I speak for many clergymen besides
myself in and around, when I say, with the utmost force
at my command, that I deplore the way in which you are
damaging the Christian cause and particularly the Church
in which you are serving as a Bishop. I fully allow your
right to your own opinions and to the expression of them,
but I do not think you are justified in taking advantage of
your position in the way that you have. I could wish that
you had been content to remain as a don in Cambridge,
where I suppose you would have been in good company. At
least there you would have been less of an embarrassment
to those who have more first hand experience of ordinary
pastoral work in the Church at home and overseas.[9]

I always thought that it was a Parson's job to get people to go to Church but if there are many [more] people like you, nobody will go.[10]

Groping, as so many of us, including yourself, obviously are for enlightenment to cure our lack of faith and moral fibre, it seems to me incomprehensible that anyone who has attained to your high clerical office should go out of his way to offend so many by such objectionable publications as your latest effort, *Honest to God*.[11]

Of course, the origins of *Honest to God* are spectacularly ordinary. The gestation of the book actually lay in completely mundane domestic accident, the kind of which could only befall Anglicans as a preface to doing something relatively radical: 'To tell you the truth I was doing nothing more strenuous than bending down to tie my shoe laces, and I got a strained back. I simply stayed in bed for three months and wrote most of the book.'[12]

Later, comedians would make much of the slipped discipline. Even so, there can be no denying that the publication of *Honest to God* in 1963 provoked the most contentious theological controversies of the late twentieth century.

The book was launched on its way by the publication of the abstract and interview in *The Observer* on the previous Sunday, under the now notorious banner headline 'Our image of God must go' – which was eye-catching, although not a headline I think that Robinson would have chosen himself. As I have already hinted, the book is a little less sharp and radical than one might suppose. Indeed, one is greeted by the ambiguity of the agenda in the preface. Robinson is at pains to acknowledge his office as a bishop and his commitment to preserving tradition and orthodoxy and to upholding the views and values of those indispensable apologists of the faith whom have gone before. At the same time, he also says that the Christian faith cannot be left there since the calling of the present is to 'far more than a restating of traditional

orthodoxy in modern terms'. This is the classic tug of war
between the theologian and the bishop, and most people now
generally agree that John Robinson, in writing *Honest to
God*, was simply thinking out loud – and sometimes not very
clearly. But the book is all the more salient for that, since he
was simply giving voice, shape and articulation to the confu-
sions and faithful doubts of many.

So, the very first chapter in *Honest to God* carries these
tensions with it – entitled as it is, 'Reluctant Revolution',
Robinson critiques the Bible's traditional three-decker universe, and yet at the same time, he is reluctant to let go of
transcendence. And so the argument proceeds with Robinson
exploring the end of theism, God as the ground of our being,
God as a person, and then in the second half of the book
exploring themes in Christology, in which he sides decisively
with Bonhoeffer, describing Jesus as the 'man for others', the
one in whose life and death love took over completely and so
was completely transparent to God. The penultimate chapter,
'The New Morality', launches a fairly straightforward attack
on commands by divine fiat as being the ground for ethics.
According to Robinson nothing is prescribed except love, a
phrase that resonates with the situational ethic that was being
powerfully espoused at the time by American theologians such
as Joseph Fletcher.

The final chapter, entitled 'Recasting the Mould', revisits the
previous arguments laid out in the book. The ambiguity that
was begun in the preface lasts until the very end. Robinson is
not promoting deism or immanentism, but rather a faith that
'grounds all reality in personal freedom – in love, and not in
determinism or mechanistic universes':[13]

> We are not rays to the sun or leaves to the tree: we are united
> to the source, sustainer and goal of our life in a relationship
> whose only analogy is that of the I to thou – except that the
> freedom in which we are held is one of utter dependence.

We are rooted and grounded wholly in love . . . It is the freedom built into the structure of our being which gives us (within the relationship of dependence) the 'distance', as it were to be ourselves. What traditional deism and theism have done is to 'objectivise' this distance into the pictorial image of a god 'out there'. But the projection of God from the world as a super-individual is no more necessary an expression of transcendence than is mileage upwards from the earth's surface. They are both but objectivications in the language of myth – in terms of 'another world' – of the transcendental, the unconditional in all our experience. The test of any restatement is not whether this rejection is preserved but whether these elements are safeguarded. And that I believe I have tried to do.[14]

As Keith Clements points out in his assessment, the book lives up to its title. Ambiguity is not meant to imply any sort of dishonesty or insincerity. That is the genius of the book. *Honest to God* is ultimately a deeply sincere book – but not very clear. It is full of Anglican fudges, gropings, questions. And the very lack of clarity says something quite profound about the nature of a church that can ask such self-critical questions within its heart, and in so doing espouse the kind of public theology that allowed many English people, many for the first time, to own their doubts as part of their questing faith. Ultimately, *Honest to God* will be mainly remembered and valued for the permission and freedom it gave to people to question their tradition and yet remain within it. As a work of theology, it is confusing and cautious in places, but ironically, it is precisely because it is *that*, that it is also radical, since it expresses the mind of a man who was both a scholar and a bishop: 'thinking out loud'.

At this point, it is probably useful to reaffirm both the distinction and unity between *traditio* (i.e., what is taught) and *tradita* (i.e., how things are taught). For example, the

American theologian George Lindbeck, among others, alerts
us to the performative aspects of doctrine. A theological
emphasis on the incarnation for example leads to a particular
style of ministry and a particular form of missiology and
Church polity. Equally, a preferred form of behaviour can
help select and shape the preferred theological fundamentals.
Exactly *how* the Church conveys its message may actually say
more about its theology than it really knows; its mode of communication can reveal hidden curricula. Or put another way,
we might say that *Honest to God* exposed the pseudoscientific
indoctrinating tendencies of the Church, and reminded people
of the difference between faith and certainty. Robinson's
style mattered as much as his substance. This was something
Dorothy Sayers had been memorably alive to in her illuminating book *Creed or Chaos?* where she satirizes a Catechism:

Q: What is faith?
A: Resolutely shutting your eyes to scientific fact.
Q: What is the human intellect?
A: A barrier to faith.
Q: What are the seven Christian virtues?
A: Respectability; childishness; mental timidity; dullness;
sentimentality; censoriousness; and depression of spirits.
Q: Wilt thou be baptised into that faith?
A: No fear.[15]

And that is the point. *Honest to God* blew the cobwebs
away. It let faith breathe and have a heartbeat of its own apart
from certainty. It did not ignore or resist the questions of the
day. It had the courage to face the present and future, and
their intellectual challenges. It was a shaky book in all kinds of
ways – which is why it was, oddly, quite robust. Because it was
not false. Robinson understood that faith was not unques-
tioning obedience, but was, rather, a refusal to settle for anything less than what is right. It put faith back in the centre of

Christian teaching by allowing some scope for doubt within the economy of theological knowledge. It gave legitimacy to questions. So the publication of *Honest to God* reminded the Church of four truths about the nature of theology that it would do well to heed in any generation.

First, theology is *public*. It is the work of groups, congregations and conversations. It is rarely the case that creeds or formulae are formed in a vacuum and designed by specific individuals, without reference to social questions and contextual pressures that are exterior to the life of the Christian community or communion. In other words, it is not at all improper to talk about doctrine being *generated* by the Church.

Second, theology is *practical*. That is to say, it explicitly sets out to discern the links between belief and behaviour, and address particular issues and concerns about the internal life of the Church and its relation to the world. People expect theology to be useful as well as contextual.

Third, theology is *plural*. That is to say, because the Church consists of a multiplicity of theologies, competing world-views, complementary convictions and more besides, the very expression of theology arises out of both unity and plurality, and its effectiveness is judged against its performative capacity to speak for more than one voice or viewpoint. The great genius of *Honest to God* is that it both unites and divides, and articulates the voices, thoughts and doubts of the silenced. To its critics, it apparently atomizes; to its champions, it unifies and frees.

Fourth, theology is *particular*. That it to say, it is specific to itself and articulates the self-conscious identity of congregations, so that they can say with one voice – even though they may mean very different things by it – 'we believe'. So there is a direct connection between the nature of theology and the purposes of theology. Critical reflection is theology's origin, context and vocation.

So in my view, *Honest to God* was not in any sense an

irresponsible work. It was, rather, a sincere and candid book, which enabled many for the first time honestly to own their private faith within the public sphere and within the Church. It opened eyes and windows, and let shafts of light come flooding in. More than anything else, it vindicates the place of theological controversy within the world of missiology. A mere 20 years later, David Jenkins would talk about the God the disturber, and would remind the Church and the public that awkward questions would be asked of us by a God who would not fit in any of our boxes. *Honest to God* made us think 40 years ago. Every generation should have its prophet. John Robinson is one such – and he is not without honour.

NOTES

1 D. L. Edwards (ed.), *The Honest to God Debate*, SCM Press, 1963, pp. 154f.
2 Edwards, *Debate*, p. 91.
3 Edwards, *Debate*, pp. 91f.
4 Edwards, *Debate*, p. 68.
5 Edwards, *Debate*, p. 68.
6 Edwards, *Debate*, p. 68.
7 Edwards, *Debate*, p. 71.
8 Edwards, *Debate*, p. 80.
9 Edwards, *Debate*, p. 51.
10 Edwards, *Debate*, p. 49.
11 Edwards, *Debate*, p. 49.
12 Quoted in Ved Mehta, *The New Theologians*, Penguin, 1968, p. 102.
13 J. A. T. Robinson, *Honest to God*, SCM Press, 1963, p. 115.
14 Robinson, *Honest to God*, p. 131.
15 D. Sayers, *Creed or Chaos*, Harcourt Brace, 1949, p. 23.

3. John Robinson and the Language of Faith in God

DON CUPITT

My knowledge of John Robinson extended over a period of 30 years. From 1952 to 1955 I was an undergraduate at Trinity Hall, and frequently attended the Clare College Eucharist then presided over by John with Bill Skelton and Charlie Moule. It embodied all the principles of the Parish Communion Movement and was the best quality Christian worship available in Cambridge at that time. Of John's lectures in the Faculty of Divinity I remember most vividly the course on *Romans* that was later published. In March 1963, when *Honest to God* appeared, I had recently succeeded John Habgood as Vice-Principal of Westcott House and was still distinctly conservative in theology. Although I did sympathize strongly with Robinson's motives in writing it, I was not deeply affected by his book. But during the 1970s, when John had returned from Southwark to Trinity College, I regularly attended a small dining club of theologians that met and talked in his rooms, and in the early 1980s when my own extreme notoriety began I was conscious of being shown much kindness by John. 'The Sixties was my decade', he said to me, 'And the Eighties will be yours' – which shows that Eric James was right to say in his biography that John loved the limelight, and had greatly enjoyed the huge publicity that surrounded him during 'his' decade.[1]

As I have said, I was not at first impressed by *Honest to God*. It seemed to be surprisingly clumsily written and obscure, and Robinson's use of the word 'God' seemed to be all over the place. He handled with confidence the Bible's mythical realism about God – the God enthroned 'up there' who is described in the language of worship – but he seemed rather ill at ease with classical Christian theism, as Herbert McCabe showed in an acute review.[2] This was odd, and at the time we put it down to the fact that John was a New Testament scholar and not a philosopher. We supposed that, like Rudolf Bultmann, he was jumping straight from the biblical world-view to the modern world-view, and neglecting the extent to which the long doctrinal and philosophical development in between had sought, and sometimes found, ways of bridging the gap. In those days of the 1950s and early 1960s there were still some formidable neo-Thomists and other exponents of classical Christian theism around. Such people's God-talk was confident and orderly enough to create a climate in which it was very possible for readers to be dismissive about *Honest to God*.

Fifteen or twenty years later, however, some of us began to see the issues very differently. In the years immediately after World War Two figures like St Thomas Aquinas and Karl Marx, Freud and Sartre had seemed to dominate the intellectual landscape. The issues of the day were debated under labels such as Catholicism, communism and secular humanism; logical positivism and existentialism; and theism, agnosticism and atheism. Now, all these names and 'positions' began to fade away, to be replaced by new names and a new agenda. Instead of talking about the clash between Catholicism and communism, we began to talk about the end of metaphysics, the Death of God and the emergence of postmodernity. And the presiding genius of the new age was Friedrich Nietzsche. At some date in the 1970s or 1980s you had to give yourself a crash course in Nietzsche: mine, I vividly remember, took place in the first half of 1981.

Among the radical theologians of the 1960s there were at least two – the Americans, Thomas J. J. Altizer and William Hamilton[3] – who had been fully aware of the importance of Nietzsche for modern theology. Their nearest counterparts in Britain were Werner and Lotte Pelz;[4] but these were, alas, rather marginal figures, and for many years Nietzsche had seemed to us too excessive and fearsome a writer to be approachable.

Gradually, however, during the late 1970s, people in Britain were beginning to wonder how far the leading thinkers of the twentieth century had all along been aware of Nietzsche and had recognized the significance of his work. The answer came as a surprise: word had indeed gone round, and during their youth many or most of the major thinkers of the German-speaking world had put in a period of study at the Nietzsche-Archive. After about 1900 the leading younger Germans somehow just knew that Nietzsche was canonical. He was someone you lived 'after', and therefore someone you had to have assimilated – *in full*. His work had made everything different, but because of his popular reputation many people drew a discreet veil over the extent of their personal debt to him. Something like this was true of thinkers as various as Freud and Jung, Heidegger and Gadamer, Thomas Mann and (amongst the theologians) at least of Albert Schweitzer, Paul Tillich, Bultmann and Bonhoeffer.

You will have noticed that the three post-Nietzschean theologians just mentioned are the very ones whose work Robinson was interpreting in *Honest to God*. And that leads me to the second point on which our view of *Honest to God* changed after 1980: belatedly, we began to realize that John Robinson was not quite as unphilosophical as we had supposed. In fact, like Albert Schweitzer, he had written his Ph.D. dissertation, *not* on a New Testament topic, but on a topic in the philosophy of religion. Schweitzer's topic was Kant's philosophy of religion – which helps us to grasp that for the rest of his life Schweitzer, following Kant, took a non-realist view of God: for him, God was just Love, a guiding spiritual ideal. Robinson's topic was Martin Buber's personalist philosophy of religion, which at that time was very influential among theologians. Like the others we have mentioned, Buber was concerned about the reconstruction of religious thought after Nietzsche, and two of his doctrines are highly relevant to our present topic.[5] First, Buber made a sharp distinction between two different ways in which we may relate ourselves to whatever we are dealing with: we may treat it as impersonal, or we may respond to and address it as utterly personal. Buber called these two attitudes *I-It* and *I-Thou*. Then second, Buber also said that we could take up the *I-Thou* attitude to Everything, at cosmic level, recognized as an eternal Thou. In such a case, according to Buber, we just *intuit* the personal: its call and our response may be unmediated by anything empirical. The eternal Thou, it was said, calls us, and can be addressed by us, but can never be described. It is always and only our Lord. We know it only as a claim upon us.

These doctrines seemed in their heyday to offer theology a vocabulary in which one could continue to talk about God, about the ultimacy of personal values, about God's self-revelation, and about personal relations between humans and God, after Nietzsche, after the end of metaphysics, and even after the end of 'realistic' or literal belief in miracles.

Such were the ideas that John Robinson adopted. They were quite common among the 'dialectical theologians' and the 'theologians of encounter' who were much read in the years just before and after World War Two, and they are very prominent in *Honest to God*. Robinson's biggest success was among the armies of people who flourished in the Welfare State's 'helping professions' – teachers, counsellors, therapists, health visitors, district nurses, social workers, probation officers and so on. These people were a new clergy, and their work was a new version of the pastoral work that in the past had been done by the parish priest and his wife. They were (roughly) post-Christian religious humanists, who were very ready to hear that to believe in God was to believe in the ultimacy of the personal, of personal values and personal relations. Personalism was *exactly* their world-view, and it was their enthusiasm for his book that buoyed Robinson up so much in the 1960s, during the years immediately following the publication of *Honest to God*.

All this is, I hope, sufficient to explain how and why our view of John Robinson's work changed around 1980 or so. The first decades after the War had been dominated by Freud and Marx, by secular humanism and socialism. Society was being reconstructed after the War, and the new professions were helping people to settle in and adjust to the welfare state, consumerism and the media society. In that context, the public naturally tended to see *Honest to God* as a work of ultra-liberal theology that cut out the supernatural and translated theological statements into statements about human relationships. The religious was the 'depth' of the interpersonal. But by the 1980s the culture had changed, and we began to see Robinson in a new way. In the manner of the Germans he admired – Tillich, Bultmann and Bonhoeffer – Robinson was trying to find a new use for God-language and a future for religious thought *after* Nietzsche and the Death of God. Society was becoming so mobile and democratic that all objective norms and realities were crumbling. This was more than just secular humanism: it was something like nihilism.

Robinson was not, as right-wingers alleged, a crazed reductionist, throwing the faith to the wolves of secularism piece by piece: *Honest to God* was his *normal* theology, and its aim was constructive. He was not discarding, he was rebuilding; and he repeatedly warns his readers that the twentieth-century crisis of faith is much graver than they yet realize. From Michael Ramsey downwards, the conservatives declared that 'John Robinson went too far', and he of course replied that posterity would probably judge that he had not gone nearly far enough. And he was obviously right.

There was however a persistent ambiguity in the message of *Honest to God*. In the end, was the book teaching a realist view of God and god-language – or was it teaching non-realism? It is hard to say, because some of Robinson's statements and arguments clearly imply a non-realist view of God, whereas in other places Robinson uses realist language that equally clearly asserts that God exists independently of human faith in him. Which was Robinson's view? It is very hard to say, because most of twentieth-century German Protestant theology – including Tillich, Bultmann and Bonhoeffer – was itself highly ambiguous on this point, because it *had* to be so, and Robinson seems to want to shelter behind that ambiguity.

I take these three points in turn. First, then, as the philosopher Alasdair MacIntyre pointed out, many of John Robinson's arguments were clearly arguments for non-realism. Unfortunately MacIntyre confuses non-realism with atheism, a mistake that continues to be common to this day, but the main point is clear enough:

[Dr Robinson] is prepared to translate theological statements into non-theological. He says that what we mean when we speak of God is 'that which concerns us ultimately'; that to speak of God is to speak of the deepest things we experience. 'Belief in God is a matter of "what you take seriously without any reservation"', and to assert that God is love is to assert the supremacy of personal relationships. All theological statements can consequently be translated into statements about human concern.[6]

Here MacIntyre is making a general point about modern Protestant theology. If you give up metaphysics, if you give up the attempt to prove the objective existence of God, then all you are left with is the 'my god' of personal religion. And the 'my god' is non-realist. He is internal to us: 'my god' is my goal in life, my spiritual ideal that I am trying to live up to, my dream, my hope. God becomes a function of human religious-ness: not a being out there, but rather the ideal towards which my faith orients me, the imaginary focus of my own spiritual project. And because MacIntyre assumes that everyone who is not a realist must be an atheist, he deduces that Robinson is an atheist.

Now it is certainly arguable that ever since Luther, Protestant faith has been of this kind – a personal religious project, oriented towards an ideal God. And it is also arguable that today, when our philosophy and our science no longer require an objectively real God out there, all of Christian faith is and has to be of the non-realist type. The word 'God' still does a job in religion, but it no longer explains events all over the place in the way it did. But as I know and you know, the churches certainly are not prepared to endorse a non-realist reading of their own faith, and John Robinson wasn't prepared to accept it either. Both in *Honest to God* and in all the subsequent debate he continued to affirm the reality of God, speaking for example of God's as 'an other reality', of 'ultimate reality as gracious', of 'the reality of Being as gracious' and so on.[7] It seems that God's reality is not limited to the sphere of human subjective religiosity, but is objective.

However, although Robinson does want to speak of the reality of God, he also says that he is not to be under-stood as attempting to reinstate the old God, the God of the philosophers. For Robinson's God doesn't *do* anything: he is not causally active. The best-remembered illustration of this is the fact that in 1983, after his cancer was diagnosed, Robinson regularly declared that he did not think of God as having *caused* the cancer, but he did believe that God could be found *in* the cancer.[8]

What did this mean? Robinson declared that God is an inescapable 'reality of life'. In all the circumstances of life, without exception, he said that he 'found himself' held in the same 'utterly personal' relationship of claim and grace. So he fell back on Buber's intuition of an eternal Thou. He calls it 'real', but he cannot spell out its reality in any way that might make sense to a philosopher.

So the ambiguity remains to the end. Robinson would (I think) have continued to claim to be a theological realist to the end of his life – without ever openly disagreeing with me – and in reply to him I would say that unless he can do something to restore metaphysics, his view doesn't and cannot differ from my own non-realism – the point being, of course, that the notion of objective 'reality' is highly metaphysical. So as I see it, the ambiguity remains and runs through all of John Robinson's work, as it runs through most of twentieth-century theology. It has some troubling consequences. One is that today's language about God very often sounds confused and unclear. For example, sometimes people talk as if the reality of God is objective and constraining, but at other times people talk as if they are aware that *they themselves* have made a moral decision about what sort of God they are going to be ready to believe in. Such talk is obvious non-realism. Sometimes people talk as if *God* gives them strength and comfort in adversity, but at other times they say that it is *their own faith* from which they derive comfort. The prophet Elijah would say to that: 'How long will you go limping with two different opinions?' (1 Kings 18.21; RSV). And he might make the same remark about the well-known and freely admitted fact that church leaders nowadays have two faiths. There is the common ecclesiastical faith to which they are institutionally committed by their office, and which they must unhesitatingly defend in public; and there is the personal faith to which they have been led by their own study and thinking. Every church leader who is theologically educated is aware of the gap between the two, and of the devices that must be used to conceal it.

John Robinson was aware of difficulties like these: they

were pressed upon him by his critics. But twentieth-century theology was not able to resolve them, and Robinson himself within four years or so (that is, by 1967) had gone as far as he could with them. Perhaps the twenty-first century will do better. We see the issues a little more clearly now than they did in the 1960s, and we see very much more clearly how late the hour is and how urgent the question of reform and renewal has become.

NOTES

1 Eric James, *A Life of Bishop John A. T. Robinson, Scholar, Pastor, Prophet*, Collins, 1987.
2 Reprinted in John A. T. Robinson and D. L. Edwards, *The Honest to God Debate*, SCM Press, 1963, pp. 165–80.
3 T. J. J. Altizer and W. Hamilton, *Radical Theology and the Death of God*, Penguin Books, 1968.
4 Werner and Lotte Pelz, *God Is No More*, Gollancz, 1963.
5 Martin Buber, *Ich und Du*, 1923; E. T. by R. Gregor Smith, T. and T. Clark, 1937.
6 Robinson and Edwards, *The Honest to God Debate*, p. 215.
7 For these phrases see especially the lecture 'Can a Truly Contemporary Person *not* be an Atheist?', 1964; reprinted in John A. T. Robinson, *The New Reformation?*, SCM Press, 1965, pp. 106–22.
8 John A. T. Robinson, *Where Three Ways Meet: Last Essays and Sermons*, SCM Press, 1987, p. 190.

4. The Language of Theism: Irony and Belief

CHRISTOPHER RYAN

To the delight of those who wished to portray him as basically a doubting Thomas, John Robinson famously gave hostages to fortune at a number of points in *Honest to God*, as, for example, in summarizing what he meant by the title of his final chapter, 'Recasting the Mould': 'It means that we have to be prepared for everything to go into the melting – even our most cherished religious categories and moral absolutes. And the first thing we must be ready to let go is our image of God himself.'[1] Yet to any fair-minded reader Robinson emerges frequently as a deeply believing Christian, whose true position is reflected in, for example, the simple statement of his own situation near the beginning of the book: 'I have never really doubted the fundamental truth of the Christian faith – though I have constantly found myself questioning its expression.'[2] The pure ring of truth likewise sounds out from the unequivocal description of the aim of the book at the end of the second chapter (devoted to answering the question posed in its title, 'The End of Theism?'): 'the task is to validate the idea of transcendence for modern man'.[3] Behind that animating urge to re-express the Christian faith lies what is possibly the book's most attractive feature: a desire to bring together fundamental elements of life that for many people are often kept apart – to unite what may be called, for want of better terms, the sacred and the secular. In Robinson's view, all too often the sacred was banished to, and circumscribed by, specifically religious events such as liturgical actions or private prayers.[4] As a result, the sacred failed to enrich, or be enriched by, the sap and vigour of daily life and the multitude of fundamental commitments embraced within it.

As the words already quoted indicate, an essential aspect of the task of bringing the two fundamental realms together is that of finding or forging a religious language that is both faithful to religion and consonant with the language used in daily life. In that sense, *Honest to God* is centrally a linguistic quest, so that one is not in the least surprised to find its author early in the book paying homage in the following terms to Paul Tillich (a German-American theologian who deeply influenced him):[5] '[His words] seemed to speak of God with and new and indestructible relevance and made the traditional language of a God that came in from outside both remote and artificial.'[6] Likewise it comes as no surprise to find Robinson, as the book draws to a close, speaking of its aim in terms of finding an 'alternative language'.[7]

What may come as a surprise, though, to anyone who rereads the book after the theological storms of the last 40 years is that he will look in vain for any *theory* of language with which to help answer the passionate desire for a new language that permeates the book. And yet the absence of any such theory is not really to be wondered at. It is true that *Honest to God* reflects a feature that, from the time of the Enlightenment at least, has characterized European theology and indeed European culture as a whole, a feature frequently characterized as 'the turn to the subject'; what holds together the various strands of argument in *Honest to God* is the view that the human being who participates in the culture of the twentieth century cannot naturally voice his deepest religious aspirations in a language that stems from a world-view that has in its non-religious aspects been discarded in the preceding several centuries. Yet, in the theological world at least, it was only in the 1970s and subsequent decades of the twentieth century that the turn to the subject focused itself specifically, intensely and highly controversially on the matter of language and on theories of language, generating the broad movement that goes under the name of 'postmodernism'. One way, then, of respecting and responding to the fundamental question posed by *Honest to God*, the way pursued in this essay, is to ask how attention to the debates on language that have characterized postmodernism can help us today to carry out anew the aim that John Robinson set himself in writing that book: the validation of the idea of transcendence for modern man – or, perhaps more strictly, postmodern man. This task, so it seems to me, has been greatly aided by the positive, yet highly discriminating, evaluation of postmodernism embodied in the theory of language in general, and of theological language in particular, put forward on Stephen Prickett's recent work, *Narrative, Religion and Science: fundamentalism versus irony, 1700–1999.*[8] I shall base the following remarks in large part on an analysis of that book (while not, of course, holding Professor Prickett responsible for the views I formulate here).

Although there may be little consensus on what exactly constitutes postmodernism, there is a widespread belief (or perhaps better, a broadly diffused feeling) that postmodernism is inimical to religious belief. This can hardly fail to be the case if one takes as integral to postmodernism the idea that the nature of knowledge is such that each subject is locked into himself and has no means of establishing truths in an objective way that can be shared by anyone other than himself, for such fundamental subjectivism entails radical pluralism and absolute relativism. If it is the case that the subject has no basis for his beliefs other than criteria of which he can be confident only that they appear to *him* to be true, then there can be as many equally valid views of the truth as there are thoughtful people seeking reasons for their beliefs. Furthermore, since in fact many reasonable people hold views that not only differ from those held by other reasonable people but actually contradict them, then all views must be deemed to be totally relative, i.e., there can be no view of which it can be said with absolute certainty that it is true. Postmodernism of this ilk we may call radical postmodernism, and there can be no doubt that postmodernism in this form excludes anything that remotely approximates to religion as this has traditionally been understood.[9]

However, one may readily embrace many of the clarifications brought about in the course of the postmodernist debate without thinking that radical postmodernism is the only or indeed the most persuasive outcome of that debate. This paper will be devoted to arguing for a twofold conclusion to the recent debates on language that shelter under the umbrella term postmodernist: that, on the one hand, theistic belief in its broad sense (belief in God who cares for his creation) is strengthened by several features of those debates; but that, on the other, the *mode* of espousing specific forms of theistic belief, the Christian among others, differs significantly from the mode of adhering to theistic belief commonly found before the end of the second millennium.

Recent debates on language have brought wide acceptance of the following key views: all evaluation of the capacity of language to embody objective truth must take into account the influence of the perceiver on what is perceived; large-scale language theory is essentially narrative in nature; it is also fundamentally ironic (a term whose meaning will shortly be discussed). These three points merit consideration in their own right before we address the specific question of how they may be thought to impinge on theistic belief.

Discussions of language in the past few decades have made it plain (or, for some, plainer than ever) that in all acts of description, even in those whose only ostensible object is some entity distinct from the person who is doing the describing, that the person or subject is in fact implicitly present in ways that profoundly affect the description.[10] Many, perhaps most, of us operate largely with what may be termed a simple physical-realist view of perception, i.e., we regard the proper operation of language in our description of the world around us as being constituted by, and exhausted by, a description of reality that ignores the subject, concentrates entirely on the object and strives to the best of its ability to represent that object in an unbiased way. Such a view of language ignores several crucial aspects of the total operation involved in finding words to represent an object. In the first place, we can only recognize an object precisely as an object if we are sufficiently aware of ourselves as discrete and individual subjects to be able to recognize that objects have an existence quite independent of our own. Famously, or infamously, young children take some time to reach knowledge of objects and of other people as independent entities, and in a real sense the psychologically immature never attain to full recognition of the independent existence and rights of other members of their species. Genuine objectivity requires a high degree of prior subjective awareness.

An equally radical dependence of objectivity on the subject is highlighted in the recognition that unless a subject possesses some fundamental mental map or perceptive grid no knowledge at all is possible for him. That is to say, when we encounter phenomena we do not merely passively register them; we have to fit them into some cognitive scheme already existing within us before we can properly take them in at all. Things have to *make sense* to us, have to fit somewhere on our mental map, if we are truly to register them at all; briefly, all perception involves interpretation. Examples of this from the visual field range from the banal to the immensely sophisticated. It has been observed, for instance, that when people unfamiliar with what a photograph is are first shown one, they merely register strange marks on a page, until they are given some minimal aid in how to represent imaginatively to themselves a three-dimensional reality on the basis of seeing patterns on a two-dimensional surface.[11] In an analogous way, Ernst Gombrich led a whole generation of art lovers to recognize that in many instances so-called primitive art forms, which seemed to be the result simply of a collective inability to portray people and objects realistically, owed their origin in fact to sophisticated modes of representing simultaneously reality as observed from different perspectives.[12] Visual art in fact exemplifies more cogently than most fields that human maturation in general, and education and professional training in particular, equip us with new ways of seeing and understanding objects and people round about us. A connected truth, as we may be reminded by encountering a keen student, is that growth in knowledge is intimately related to the degree of mental activity that the knower brings to the data in hand: perception and knowledge are in fact the result of a dynamic encounter between the knower and what is to be known, rather than (as we often assume) a mere impression made by what is known on a passive knower.[13] In broader cultural terms, we may say that recent debates have served to establish or reinforce the view that a central function of the creative artist in any field is to introduce us to new ways of seeing and knowing.

Acceptance of the importance of the subject, and so of the limitations imposed on knowledge both by factors individual to the knower and by the state of the science and culture of the time, requires as a corollary that to a very great extent all knowledge is subject to revision in the light of ongoing discoveries. Recognition of these severe limitations will entail for many of us, perhaps rather painfully, a humbler evaluation of the degree of truth we possess than that to which we have become accustomed: it is incumbent upon all to acknowledge that, measured against the infinity of the knowable and the multitude of those who know, as individuals and as societies ours can have only a very partial grasp of the truth, and other

individuals and societies will have a valid perception of reality
that differs from our own. To the educated person today, cultural and cognitive pluralism is an ineradicable fact of life, to
be lamented in that it bespeaks in all of us a woeful ignorance
and perhaps a regrettable parochialism, to be welcomed in
that it signals recognition that some of the truth that is greater
than ourselves is already possessed and enjoyed by others.

Acknowledgement of the highly subjective nature of knowledge readily coheres with acceptance of another conclusion
to be drawn from recent studies of language, namely, that all
large-scale theories about the nature of man must in the final
analysis be narrative in form.[14] This conclusion follows from
two simple observations. The human race as a whole is obviously and inescapably historical, and any theory that purports
to describe human nature must make sense of the history that
is common to all who possess that nature. What holds of the
race in general is true also of the individuals which make it
up: answers to such questions as 'who am I?' or 'how does
my life make sense?' can be answered truly only by a response
that takes into account the growth and decline to which each
of us is subject, and the vagaries that each of us must encounter
and deal with at the various stages which mark the life cycle.
Simple as these observations may be, one important aspect
of the truth they embody can easily be overlooked: basic
scientific theories about man are also historical, also 'tell a
story'. Attention has recently been drawn to the fact that large-
scale scientific theories touching on the nature and destiny of
the human race frequently make use of personal terms and
of figures of speech such as metaphor and simile, which are
the hallmark of narrative accounts but which can easily be
thought to be more or less excluded in principle by all science
as such. An analysis of the language of Darwin's theory of
evolution, for example, perhaps the most widely accepted and
best known of the scientific theories that touch on man, will
readily make clear that Darwin frequently portrays nature as

if it were purposive and acted in ways similar to an intelligent agent;[15] indeed Darwin himself recognized that he did, almost in spite of himself: 'For brevity's sake I sometimes speak of natural selection as an intelligent power . . . I have, also, often personified the word Nature; for I have found it difficult to avoid this ambiguity.'[16] More broadly still, one recognizes instantly, when it is drawn to our attention, that perhaps the most basic category of all scientific description, that of 'law' (as in 'the laws of nature'), is, in fact, a term that properly and originally belongs to personal discourse: laws, strictly speaking, entail a lawgiver. All large-scale theories of man are, then, necessarily grand narratives, i.e., theories that purport to give a basic historical account of how human nature has evolved, which seem necessarily to be couched in language that strictly and properly belongs to personal agency.

A third conclusion flows from the above two: that the language of all grand narrative accounts must be ultimately 'ironic' in mode (to adopt a term championed by Stephen Prickett).[17] Irony in this context means two things. It signifies, first, that the language of grand narrative can describe only indirectly the basic reality underlying the universe; the ultimate ground or explanation of the universe will be hidden, and can be captured in human language only imperfectly and at one remove, in language that has been coined to describe finite beings in general, and human beings in particular. Second, when we refer to that ultimate ground of being we will be *aware* that our language is only imperfect: we shall say one thing, but recognize that in a fundamental way we are also saying something else, or rather we shall recognize that what we say necessarily entails something that we cannot say, cannot capture in words. This conclusion follows from the first two characteristics described. If human description is necessarily limited and partial, and what we are trying to describe goes beyond the limited and the partial, then we necessarily speak of what lies beyond in a way that indicates awareness of what we cannot say granted the nature of human speech. We are drawn to this conclusion likewise by the narrative quality of all theory, as reflection on the novel, the narrative genre par excellence, can readily show. Narrative that touches upon the most profound of human emotions and aspirations, such as personal love, complete justice, and ineluctable tragedy, always has recourse to a variety of figures of speech that indicate that it can at best approximate to what it seeks to describe. To speak of what is deepest not just to individuals but to the human race as a whole requires that we embrace figures of speech, and adopt a fundamental indirectness.[18] If we are to be even partially true to the wealth of reflection on human nature that has been manifested in a huge range of societies and can never be fully captured by any one language or culture, then all grand narratives must be aware that they speak only partially and indirectly – in a word, ironically.

What, then, are some of the main implications for theology and theism of what may be termed a grand-narrative view of language? If, as has been argued above, language in its description of man and his situation is primarily a storytelling or narrative activity, then God cannot be a direct object of language in its primary mode: the only evident agents in the world in which the human story evolves are either totally or partially physical. However, since the human being is partially suprasensible, in that he can exercise reason, God's existence may be deduced by the human being using the rational powers that he commands. The mode of man's possible knowledge of God will be discussed later, but two of its basic features should be noted here, as following immediately from what has just been stated. On the one hand, it is in man's *rational* and publicly accountable knowledge that God can be approached only indirectly. This leaves open the possibility of there being quasi-immediate knowledge of God on the part of some individuals, that is particular and private to them, or to the specific religious community to which they belong. On the other hand, one ought not to restrict the rational knowledge of God that is available to all human beings to knowledge that is logically compelling. As Newman spelled out at some length over a century ago (especially in his discussion of the illative sense in *The Grammar of Assent*),[19] and as many scientists today readily acknowledge in describing their professional activity, in a great many fundamental areas of life human beings rightly content themselves with a practical certainty that is based only on a rational probability. From data that, in a strictly logical sense, point no more than probably towards a particular conclusion, we must all in very many important areas of our lives extrapolate to an unperturbed acceptance of that conclusion as being for all practical purposes certain. In the supremely important area of knowledge of God, then, we need not find it strange that in the religious sphere we can attain only to faith which is based on probabilities, since in doing so we are using a process analogous to one that is operative in much of the rest of our lives.

A believer of the grand-narrative type, reviewing the story of man and his world, finds in the public and rational sphere three major features that persuade him of the existence of God. All three are based on the same logical pattern: since in any sphere of activity that can have its origin in the human being the presence of a high degree of intelligibility in a series of actions argues for those actions having had their source in human intelligence rather than their having come about through pure chance, so also in spheres of reality that cannot owe their origin to human beings the presence of a high degree of intelligibility argues for the existence of a Creator, i.e., a rational being with the power to bring about such intelligently patterned actions.

For many of us, perhaps indeed for most, the immediate impression made by the world we live in is not conducive to belief in God. Such patterns as we discern in our daily lives are to a great extent the result of very hard work on the part of others and of ourselves, and much of the information brought to us through the media from beyond our daily lives speaks of suffering on huge scale. Some of this suffering is certainly attributable at one or more removes to preventable evil human actions, but much of it arises inescapably from phenomena over which no human beings have control. Against this unpromising background, however, there are basic arguments that weigh the scales in favour of God's existence. The degree of patterning, of sheer intelligibility, in the world around and beyond us is breathtaking, from the structure of subatomic particles to the expansion of the universe. We often take for granted the characterization of our era as the age of science, without reflecting that the wonders of science are possible only because the world which science studies is wonderfully susceptible of rational analysis.[20] As one scientist has put it, it is nothing less than astounding that it is the ever-increasing complexities of mathematical reasoning, that most sophisticated of rational activities, which is an indispensable tool for revealing to us the secrets of nature.[21]

What holds true for the object, the multi-patterned world around us, holds also for the subject, the one observing; and that in several ways. We are aware of the stupendously patterned variety around us only because we are the kind of being capable of discovering and entertaining that complexity through a receptivity and creativity that matches the complexity of the world which forms the object of our thought. Moreover, accustomed though we have long been to admiring the wonders of the human mind and the brain in which its activities originate, it has taken until the latter part of the twentieth century to make us aware of quite how highly and individually patterned is the basic structure of each human being, through the cracking of the DNA code. This further ground for wonder is complemented by the recently acquired awareness of how finely tuned the physical conditions of a planet have to be before life may appear on it, conditions whose simultaneous existence is theoretically so unlikely that their actual presence strongly suggests the existence also of a Creator able to bring about this totally improbable conjunction of circumstances.[22]

A third strand of argument in favour of theism arises from recognizing in the process of knowing itself a fundamentally fiduciary quality.[23] Few would quarrel with the view that in our early years the urge to know is largely fulfilled by taking on faith the word of countless people. What is perhaps less recognized is that in adult life this faith in other people's word operates not only in day-to-day living, where no one can pretend to have first-hand knowledge of all fields, but also in those areas in which one does have specific, personal expertise: what one can personally verify, discover or negate in any given area of professionalism is miniscule compared to the data we take on trust in setting about our own endeavours. Less recognized still is the view that (according to the line of argument adopted here) in seeking to broaden and deepen our knowledge we operate with a basic faith in reality itself, indeed with, subjectively, an infinite faith in reality which corresponds, objectively, to an infinity in reality itself. The move from the dependence of childhood to the maturity of adulthood undoubtedly has as one of its principal motors the cultivation of the urge to 'find out for ourselves'; this we do by regularly checking our personal beliefs against some commonly accepted reality. If we are to gain expertise in a particular field, we aim to make ourselves master of that area to the best of our ability by a knowledge that commands as much of the reality of the area concerned as we can. We may have bright ideas, but they are of little use until they undergo what is at times referred to somewhat roughly as 'a reality-check'. There is, then, a process of discarding ideas that do not have adequate grounding in reality, and the adopting of ideas that are properly grounded. Put otherwise, we recurrently find that the particular area of reality with which we are dealing has further intelligibility and meaning. If we reflect on that process of discovery we recognize that it is fuelled, receives its energy, from a twofold source: an urge within us to know, and the presence in objective reality of ever-broadening areas of intelligibility. The urge to know is without limit, and since, as was noted above, that urge is regularly fulfilled, there is prima facie a case for believing that the objective reality that recurrently matches and fulfils that urge is likewise without limit. It is, in other words, quite reasonable to believe that to our infinite desire to know there corresponds an infinite being.[24]

It should be noted that the process of knowing, which by its regular finding of fulfilment suggests the existence of infinite being, has broadly speaking two basic forms, which may be termed scientific and aesthetic. The scientific consists of the steady accumulation of knowledge in a given area that gradually and patiently builds up a recognized body of knowledge, though one that is capable of indefinite expansion. The aesthetic consists of the encounter with being through beauty that often has about it a speed and an immediacy that on the one hand opens, however fleetingly and indeterminately, on to infinite vistas, and on the other directs us towards reorienting our lives in a deeper and less self-preoccupied way.

How might one characterize belief held on the above grounds, that is, belief that tries to take with full seriousness major developments in contemporary culture, yet squarely aligns itself with the theistic? Strange as it may sound at first, a helpful and apt term for such belief is ironic, as discussed on pages 53–4. Applying this term to religious belief, we may say that two things are meant: first, that belief of the kind described is necessarily formulated in a way that leaves the object of the belief more hidden than revealed, granted the discrepancy between the infinity of the divine and the finite mind that professes belief in it; second, that the person professing the belief is keenly aware of the discrepancy between the two, and recognizes fully that he worships a largely hidden God.[25]

What are some of the principal characteristics implied in such a mode of belief in God? I would suggest five. First, ironic belief is at its core quietly confident. Quietude is required principally because one recognizes that very many people of the utmost moral and intellectual integrity do *not* find the grounds of belief adequate, however persuasive they may seem to oneself; put otherwise and rather bluntly, one accepts that though the grounds of one's belief are sufficient for oneself they are not in any universal sense rationally compelling.[26] And, if one is honest, one acknowledges that there are times (more frequent and more intense in some people than in others) when the grounds for calling in question the acceptance of a divine and loving being as the source of our world become all too evident, and overwhelm one's own belief. Yet confidence is the dominant mode of one's belief, a belief which constantly re-emerges to permeate one's life, and which can at least on occasion intensify to the point of profound and unclouded gladness.

Ironic belief is, second, generously pluralistic in religious matters.[27] We in the West live in an era when for the first time all the major religions of the world are becoming part of the normal daily awareness of the world around us. Until our societies have learned to live with and evaluate these hitherto culturally strange religions we shall not be in a position to discriminate just how far they differ from our own; the ironic believer will in any case be predisposed to discover that non-Christian religions have insights presently foreign to us that are important and life-enhancing. Even within the Christian religion, the ironic believer will recognize that it has been painfully clear at least since the end of the first millennium with regard to Eastern and Western Christianity, and from the sixteenth century as regards Western Christianity itself, that no single interpretation of the Christian grand narrative has been able to command the assent of all Christians, far less that of society as a whole.[28] Ironic belief, then, views the diversity in religious belief in the world as stemming in large measure from the diversity of ways in which the infinite can legitimately be approached, and no less from the inability of the human mind fully to grasp the infinite.

A third characteristic of the ironic mode of belief follows directly: a ready acceptance of religious pluralism entails that one must regard one's own belief system as being profoundly open to modification and enrichment by other forms of belief. Such a stance denotes freedom, not total relativism. As an individual, the Christian ironic believer will have roots sufficiently deep in theism to be able to view doctrinal challenges from other religions as an opportunity for development rather than a danger. He will recognize also, however, that he can best flourish within his own Christian tradition when the solitude of intellectual questioning and private prayer are nourished by the shared liturgical life of a Christian community, though necessarily one which is respectful of the need for radical religious questioning.[29] (The same may be said, of course, *mutatis mutandis*, regarding those in other communities of belief.)

A fourth characteristic of ironic belief, making religious belief itself possible in a highly pluralistic world, is a much stronger emphasis on the apophatic than was generally the case heretofore for Christians. From its earliest years, as the New Testament Letters make clear, and as is manifest in the Jewish culture which it inherits, the Christian Church has recognized that human words must fail in the description of the divine, and that an essential element of the human being's attitude to God must be silence in the face of mystery. Recognition of this basic truth has not, however, prevented the Church from being through the ages so confident of the degree to which it can precisely formulate the Christian message as often to show quite inadequate recognition of the profundity of the divine mystery and the poverty of human speech. Today's ironic Christian believer will want continually to recognize the limits of human understanding of, and speech about, the divine in his own life and in that of his church.[30]

Despite the caveats demanded by sensitivity to the limits of language and by acknowledgement of the magnitude of mystery, the ironic believer will, nonetheless, want last, but by no means least, to insist that he is a theistic realist.[31] He will want to make clear that between the use of religious language to refer to the deity, however obscurely known, and the use of that language simply to express the depth and range of the emotions of the human being, there is an infinite difference. One can be fully understanding of a Christian whose intellectual journeying or bitter experience has led him to rejection of belief in God but also to a desire to retain and make use of the language of his old belief, just as one can be respectful of any non-believer who finds solace in making use of religious language to express his feelings or imaginings. This does not imply, though, assenting to the view that language is being used in fundamentally the same sense by both non-realist and realist. An ironic believer will hold that as a matter of fact something suprahuman is hidden, and that that something, God, differs infinitely from the believer and his many needs and emotions.

Before leaving the topic of the mode of the believer's knowledge of God one ought to note that, in the ironic believer's view of faith, a certain privileged status is to be accorded to beauty as a means of access to the divine.[32] It is crucial for any educated believer that his belief should rest in part on reasoned arguments drawn from the study of nature that may broadly be called philosophical. Without such reasoned arguments the believer's faith is not integrated with his deductive power, and rests entirely on his power of intuition, thus at least leaving the human being unhealthily split in his highest capacity, the intellect, and at worst rendering his belief unhappily fragile.

However, although the object of belief based on reasoned arguments is recognized to be personal, the establishing of a personal relationship with that being is exceptionally difficult since philosophical argument necessarily involves knowledge of him at one remove, the direct object being a finite being and the infinite object being that which is known indirectly through the existence of the finite being. The psychological distance between the finite and the infinite when the latter is known through an aesthetic experience is less marked: in being enraptured by finite beauty the believer senses simultaneously the infinite that permeates and sustains that finite beauty and the world in which it exists. It seems a matter of common sense to recognize further that, broadly speaking, the capacity for aesthetic experience is more widely found in society than is the ability to engage in close philosophical reasoning.

The attitude of the ironic believer can further be clarified if we also address specifically the question of how ironic belief is to be differentiated from other attitudes to theism. The ironic believer would first of all wish to register his dissent from those who roundly declare that from the evidence publicly available the truth about God is *obvious*, whether the truth be that he does exist or does not exist.[33] As has been noted, it is central to the ironic form of belief to emphasize that, as far as evidence that belongs to the public realm is concerned, God is known only indirectly and his nature remains more hidden than revealed. Assertions that God plainly does or does not exist (often accompanied by a strident rhetoric) necessarily entail the view that those who disagree with such assertions are either intellectually ill equipped or wilfully blind; they are, in short, either stupid or immoral. To the ironic believer such an assertive stance does not do justice to the complexity of the evidence for and against God's existence, or to the intelligence and character of the majority of people on both sides of the theistic divide. If an assertive Christian believer were to counter in response that God's existence is clear to those to whom he gives his grace, then the ironic believer would reply that either such a grace is offered only to some and not to others, in which case it cannot be said properly speaking to be in the public realm, or it is offered to all and rejected by many, in which case the view is no answer to the charge of implying large-scale moral deficiency among unbelievers.

The difference between the ironic theist and both the agnostic and the non-assertive theist is in important ways less than that which separates him from the assertive advocates of theism and of non-theism alike, although the difference is hardly insignificant. With both the agnostic and the non-assertive theist, the ironic believer will share the view that there are rational criteria for assessing the truth or otherwise of basic assertions about the world and about God. He will likewise share with both the view that, rationally speaking, the evidence for or against the existence of God is to some degree ambivalent; he will, consequently, regard it as part of our common lot that there be an element of rational uncertainty about our views regarding the ultimate meaning of human existence and the possibility for humanity of eternal life and perfect happiness. That said, there remains, of course, an immense divide between the ironic believer and the agnostic and non-theist, for the ironic believer thinks that the evidence weighs decidedly in favour of belief in God.

Through that belief, the position of the ironic believer approximates to that of the assertive theist, but it is worth stressing both aspects of the word 'approximates'. The ironic believer is close to the assertive believer in that, broadly speaking at least, both share a substantive belief in God, the transcendentally most important of all beings. What makes the position of the ironic believer only *close* to the assertive believer is a matter of style, where this is to be understood as something fundamental in human life, as signalled in the dictum: 'le style c'est l'homme.' A respectful caution in the manner of holding and presenting one's theistic belief that allows one fully to respect non-believers is close to the heart of the ironic believer.

The point may be pressed by considering finally one of the most profound questions regarding religious belief (one not raised, in fact, by Prickett): why has God willed that we should live in such darkness as believers? Why is his presence not so manifest in the world as to leave no serious ground for denying it? Short of the beatific vision, we shall lack the means of answering that question definitively, but one line of thought is worth pursuing here, tentative though the pursuit must be. The answer to the question posed is twofold: first, religious faith (and not quasi-sight) is apt with regard to God because it is by a corresponding moral faith that we operate in the realm of ethics; secondly, the ethical realm has a certain priority over the theistic. Let us take Dante's *Divine Comedy* as a means of teasing out these points; doing so will allow dissent from the interpretation that, as he brings his very considerable achievement in *Narrative, Religion and Science* to a close, Prickett gives to a key episode in that work, namely, Dante's entry to the Earthly Paradise. At least for the majority of us, there is no foundation for the principles of ethics other than the rightness with which those principles appeal immediately to us. Adherence to ethical principles is, essentially, a matter of faith: they are essentially self-justifying.[34] This attitude is reflected at the centre of the *Comedy* when Virgil instructs Dante the pilgrim with respect to the instinctive regard (*affetto*) in which the human being holds the highest goods (*i primi appetibili*) that underlie the power of free choice.[35] Speaking of the human mind in general, Virgil declares:

> [The human being] has a proper power given to it, of which it is not aware unless that power is active; its presence can be discerned only when it is actually in operation, as life is in a plant when green leaves show.[36]

Virgil goes on immediately to talk of the distinctive powers of intellect and will within the mind:

> And so man does not know whence comes knowledge of the first principles, nor whence comes regard for the highest goods, which are at work in you as is the instinct in bees to make honey.[37]

It is quite reasonable to hold (provided that one is not a determinist) that the principles of the moral life *should* be self-justifying rather than rationally compelling, for this is a condition of the freedom of the will. The same holds true for the act of religious faith. It is right that for faith good grounds can be found, but not rationally compelling ones, for otherwise faith, like the adherence to moral principles, would not be free. There is, in other words, an aptness attaching to the modal parity of holding moral principles and holding a religious creed; ultimately, both moral principles and religion are founded in faith.

There is, furthermore, a certain priority to be given to morality. Again the point may be made from the *Comedy*, this time *pace* Prickett. It will be recalled that when Dante reaches the Earthly Paradise at the top of Mount Purgatory, Virgil disappears and, entirely contrary to Dante's expectations, the Beatrice whom the pilgrim then encounters is far from meltingly loving and is in fact distant and scornful: she asks sarcastically what he is doing on the mountain, in terms that leave no doubt that she holds him unworthy to be there.[38] Prickett interprets this setback for the pilgrim to mean that everything that had occurred to Dante in his journey to that point has proved to be of no avail: '[Virgil] unexpectedly disappears, leaving Dante bereft of support, to find that everything he has so far learned, and which has got him to the Earthly Paradise, is valueless.'[39] This is seriously to misread the poem, and to underplay the importance of free choice for Dante. Such an interpretation has in effect to ignore, among much else, the incision of seven Ps on Dante's forehead by the angel custodian at the start of the pilgrim's journey up the mountain (the seven Ps representing the seven capital sins, as indicated in *Purgatorio* 9), and to take no serious account of the removal of those Ps one by one as the pilgrim progresses from ledge to ledge, witnessing the horror of each sin and the beauty of its opposite virtue. In his meeting with Beatrice and his need for further repentance, Dante the pilgrim is to be understood rather as a means used by Dante the poet of calling attention to the crucial point that despite the rigours of his journey, and the removal of the Ps, the pilgrim's acknowledgement of the evil of sin had remained largely theoretical, and not applied to himself. What Beatrice wishes from him before he can properly take his place in the Earthly Paradise, and thereafter in Paradise proper, is a full repentance that betokens acceptance of complete, individual responsibility for his own evil deeds. Beatrice is, in other words, emphasizing the importance of free choice and morality, not discounting it. Granted, then, the opening of the poem, with its portrayal of the virtuous pagans, the presence of Virgil all the way to the Earthly Paradise, and the excoriation by Beatrice of Dante for his moral weakness as a prelude to his being worthy of heaven, the poem suggests that moral choice is in a real and important way independent of faith and even antecedent to it.

To apply this lesson to the case in hand, one is drawn to conclude that religious belief must go hand in hand with morality, must be nurtured by it and indeed must in a real sense be secondary to it. This attitude is at the very least in danger of being overridden by the espousal of an assertive faith, which can readily fail to respect the non-believer in his independent status as a human being. Respect for humanity, one's own and others, is best safeguarded and nourished when the belief with which one may be blessed gives full rein to the irony inherent to it this side of heaven.

NOTES

1 J. Robinson, *Honest to God*, SCM Press, 1963, p. 124.
2 Robinson, *Honest to God*, p. 24.
3 Robinson, *Honest to God*, p. 44.
4 One must assume that this view found an echo in the hearts and minds of the countless people who have bought his book.
5 Robinson was particularly influenced by Tillich's *The Shaking of the Foundations*, SCM Press, 1949.
6 Robinson, *Honest to God*, p. 22.
7 Robinson, *Honest to God*, p. 132.
8 S. Prickett, *Narrative, Religion and Science: Fundamentalism Versus Irony, 1700–1999*, Cambridge University Press, 2002. For a historical review of 'the turn to the subject', see Prickett, *Narrative*, pp. 94–127. On postmodernism, see especially Prickett, *Narrative*, pp. 15–53. Strangely, in what has come to be called the postmodernist debate, little attention has been given to the exploration of language as a rule-bound game in the English analytical school of the mid-twentieth century, a debate given focus and some notoriety by A. J. Ayer's *Language, Truth and Logic*, Victor Gollancz, 1946. The point is noted by Prickett, *Narrative*, p. 180. For a fuller account of modernism and theology, see G. Hyman, *The Predicament of Postmodern Theology*, Westminster John Knox Press, 2001.
9 Prickett, *Narrative*, outlines many of the religiously negative aspects of postmodernism in Chapter 1, and returns to challenge them directly in Chapters 6–7.
10 This theme is discussed at some length in Prickett, *Narrative*, pp. 54–93.
11 Prickett, *Narrative*, p. 90.
12 See especially his *Art and Illusion: A Study in the Psychology of Pictorial Representation*, Pantheon Books, 2nd edn, 1960. Prickett, *Narrative*, discusses the work on pp. 88–90.
13 Prickett frequently returns to the theme that learning involves an attitude of creativity, not merely of passivity: see especially *Narrative*, pp. 93 and 236–9.
14 On narrative as a key modern category, see especially Prickett, *Narrative*, pp. 14–46 and 107–14.
15 See especially Prickett, *Narrative*, pp. 26–31, and 78–80.
16 Darwin, *The Variation of Animals and Plants*, John Murray, 1875, pp. 7–8; quoted in Prickett, *Narrative*, p. 30.
17 The theme of irony threads Prickett, but see especially the discussion on *Narrative*, p. 75 of how the author understands the term 'irony', and his extended treatment of the topic on pp. 81–93 and 195–224.

18 On the striking evidence presented by J. Gilligan in his study, *Violence: Reflections on our deadliest epidemic*, G. P. Putnam, 1996; see Prickett, *Narrative*, pp. 229–34.

19 First published 1870, new edition by I. Ker, Clarendon Press, 1985.

20 See especially Prickett, *Narrative*, pp. 225–6.

21 'The miracle of the appropriateness of the language of mathematics for the formulation of the laws of physics is a wonderful gift which we neither understand nor deserve', E. Wigner: 'The unreasonable effectiveness of mathematics in the natural sciences', *Communications on Pure and Applied Mathematics*, 13, 1960, pp. 1–14; quoted by Prickett, *Narrative*, p. 251. For a sympathetic and sensitive account of the relation between science and religion, see the work of A. Peacocke, notably *Paths from Science towards God: The end of all our exploring*, Oneworld, 2001.

22 See Prickett, *Narrative*, pp. 250–1.

23 This theme is discussed at length in Prickett, *Narrative*, pp. 157–94, where the author draws extensively on the work of J. H. Newman, M. Polanyi, and G. Steiner. Steiner's views gained widespread attention through his *Real Presences*, Faber, 1989.

24 If we add that, as has just been discussed, the objective reality we know and the type of beings we are as knowers reveal themselves as of such astounding complexity as to make their random occurrence highly unlikely, then that prima facie case is markedly confirmed.

25 Auden captures the mood of irony often struck in modern religious literature. See Prickett, *Narrative*, p. 45.

26 On uncertainty in one's deepest beliefs, see Prickett, p. 75.

27 Prickett champions pluralism as 'part of the very fabric of existence' (*Narrative*, p. 259). In the context of the study of world religions, notable champions of a generous religious pluralism have been (among others) Ninian Smart (e.g., in *The Religious Experience of Mankind*, Scribner, 1969; and John Hick (in, e.g., *An Interpretation of Religion*, Macmillan, 1989).

28 A summary of the effect of the religious wars connected with the Reformation and its aftermath is given in Prickett, *Narrative*, pp. 128–35. On the pluralism of beliefs that marked the Reformation and Counter-Reformation see C. Lindberg, *The European Reformations*, Blackwell, 1989; and *The Reformation Theologians*, Blackwell, 2002; and D. MacCulloch, *The Reformation: Europe's house divided, 1490–1700*, Allen Lane, 2003.

29 The importance of what might be termed 'rooted pluralism' has long been championed by a pioneer in the study of world religions, W. C. Smith: see, e.g., *The Meaning and End of Religion*, Macmillan, 1962; and *Towards a World Theology*, Macmillan, 1981.

30 For some recent examples of attempts to rethink the Christian message without jettisoning essentials see P. Badham, *The Contemporary Challenge of Modernist Theology*, University of Wales Press, 1998; J. Jobling and I. Markham, eds, *Theological Liberalism: Creative and Critical*, SPCK, 2000; M. J. Langford, *A Liberal Theology for the Twenty-First Century: A passion for reason*, Ashgate, 2001; M. D. Chapman, ed., *The Future of Liberal Theology*, Ashgate, 2002.

31 See Prickett, *Narrative*, pp. 195–224.

32 See Prickett, *Narrative*, pp. 207–24, 249–50, and 259–60.

33 This theme is implicit in the central notion of irony in Prickett, and indeed runs throughout the work.

34 How those principles are applied in particular cases can, of course, be a matter of grave dispute.

35 It is no accident that Dante the poet has so constructed his poem that it is a non-Christian who gives instruction of this kind.

36 'specifica vertute ha in se colletta, / la qual sanza operar non e sentita, / ne si dimostra mai che per effetto, / come per verdi fronde in pianta vita' (*Purg.* 18.51–4).

37 'Pero, la onde vegna lo 'ntelletto / de le prime notizie omo non sape, / e de' primi appetibili l'affetto, / che sono in voi si come studio in ape / di far lo mele' (*Purg.* 18.55–9).

38 'Do look at me. Indeed I am, indeed I am Beatrice; how have you deigned to approach the mountain? Did you not know that man is happy here?' ('Guardaci ben! Ben son, ben son Beatrice; / come degnasti d'accedere al monte? / Non sapei tu che qui e l'uom felice?': *Purg.* 30: 73–5).

39 Prickett, *Narrative*, p. 249; the point is made again at pp. 259–60. The author puts forward this interpretation at greater length in *Romanticism and Religion*, Cambridge University Press, 1976, pp. 211–23.

5. *Honest to God* and the Dangerous Ethic

PETER J. GOMES

For a book to do well with a British public, it was once considered an infallible rule that it must involve religion, royalty and sex; and a teaser for such a book might be this: ' "Take your hand off my knee," said the duchess to the bishop.' Two out of three is not bad, and John A. T. Robinson, without the assistance of royalty, sold over one million copies of his little book that was translated into 17 languages. A bishop writing on theology was hardly news, and almost as dull as a theologian writing on theology, but this was no ordinary bishop. John Robinson enjoyed a solid, if not exciting, reputation as a biblical scholar, and when he wrote this book he was a part of what was then called 'South Bank Religion', a progressive, even activist, social gospel emanating from London's 'other' cathedral, Southwark, on the wrong side of the Thames and under the charismatic and frenetic leadership of Mervyn Stockwood. What created the 'buzz', as we now say, about Robinson, was not only the fact that he was raising questions about the faith that he as a bishop was sworn to defend, but that he came to this discussion already widely known as the 'Lady Chatterley Bishop'. Hence the sex, and two-thirds of the infallible formula for, if not success, then notoriety.

An effort had been made to declare D. H. Lawrence's novel

Lady Chatterley's Lover as obscene, and John A. T. Robinson, consecrated barely one year, gave evidence in defence of the novel, arguing that in Lawrence's view the adultery between her ladyship and her gardener was an act of holy communion. The prosecution failed, Robinson became something of a celebrity, and he earned a rebuke from the Archbishop of Canterbury, Geoffrey Fisher, who felt that his participation in the trial had given offence to many ordinary Christians and was a profound mistake. That was in 1960. Three years later, in 1963, the 'Lady Chatterley Bishop' would write *Honest to God*, which, among other things, would earn another archiepiscopal rebuke, this one from Michael Ramsey, who said:

> It is utterly wrong and misleading to denounce the imagery of God held by Christians, men, women, and children: imagery that they have got from Jesus himself, the image of God the Father in heaven, and to say that we can't have any new thought until it is all swept away.[1]

I well remember reading *Honest to God* when I was an undergraduate in college. One of our professors in the religion department had told us that we should read it and, as I was a dutiful undergraduate, I did. I remember my initial reaction: 'What's all the fuss?' Having read Bonhoeffer, Bultmann and Tillich in the basic survey course Religion 101, there was little in Robinson's synopsis of the twentieth-century theological response to modernity to surprise or overwhelm me. Then again, I was required to read this stuff, for I was thinking about the ministry and theological school, and this was essential material. Quickly, however, my reaction became one of relief, and even of encouragement, for here was a bishop, and an English bishop at that, writing of his honest concerns about things that had been of some concern to me.

At that time I had left the sheltering convictions of my lukewarm evangelical upbringing, and the collegiate study of

religion had not provided me with any new certainties. I loved
the faith, but I felt estranged from it: my heart said 'Yes', but
my increasingly well-trained undergraduate mind said 'No',
and I was not far removed from the pursuit of a secular profes-
sion. I remembered my father's remark when as a young boy I
had told him that I wanted to become a minister, and he had
paused in the conversation, creating an awkward silence, and
then had said simply, 'I had always hoped my son would do
honest work.' Now here was a man, John Robinson, of stellar
intellectual and ecclesiastical credentials, who was attempting
in his book of 141 pages to do honest work. As we said in
those days, he spoke to my condition.

Many years later I had a chance to tell John Robinson just
what his book had meant to me. I had been at Harvard for
more than a decade, and was about to enjoy two terms of
sabbatical leave at Emmanuel College, Cambridge; Robinson
had spent time at Harvard before my time, and he still had
friends there, some of whom were now my colleagues. A letter
of introduction was duly dispatched from one of them on my
behalf, and when I arrived at Emmanuel I found a cordial note
awaiting me from the Dean of Trinity College, inviting me to
take dinner with him in Hall as soon as I was able. We fixed
upon a day, and off I went to meet the famous bishop. He could
not have been nicer to me. The evening, as it turned out, was a
rather special evening at Trinity, since earlier in the day one of
its most famous old boys, Prince Charles, had announced his
engagement to Lady Diana Spencer. The Master had called for
special claret, and the royal health was drunk. John Robinson
and I, however, did not remain long in the company of the
Fellows, retiring instead to the Dean's rooms to talk. He was
lively and engaging, and invited me to join his small group of
colleagues and friends who met on Tuesday nights to do what
he called 'fringe theology'. All went well until I began to tell
him how grateful I was for *Honest to God*, how it had come
to me at just the right time and had probably preserved me,

and many others, for the ministry. I was perhaps too effusive
– I even felt like an autograph hound or a stage-door Johnny
– and his silence did nothing to help relieve my mounting
anxiety. Then he said, more in sorrow than in anger, 'That
book is the worst thing I ever did.' I should have kept silent
but I protested. He cut me off, saying something to the effect
that he had done many good things for the Church and the
university, had published serious books, had taken pleasure
in his work as priest and don, but that he would forever be
known, alas, as '*Honest to God* Robinson'. I tried to change
the subject, but the glory had departed from the evening and
as soon as I could decently do so, so did I. We met many more
times over the course of that lovely spring of 1981, but I never
mentioned the book again, and nor did he. It was only after
I had read Eric James's quite masterful biography of John A.
T. Robinson, published not long after Robinson's death, that
I began to understand something of what had happened that
evening, and of the burden that the book must have been to
him over the years.

Yet, what may well have been a burden to him proved a
blessing to me, and never more so than when I look back over
the past 30 years of my own professional career as a professor of divinity and Preacher to Harvard University, trying to
make sense of the Christian religion in a community of cul-
tured despisers, where people believe either too much or too
little. No one ever said that honest work was either easy or
appreciated, but my work would be all the more difficult were
it not for John Robinson's honest hard work.

That notwithstanding, Robinson recognized the problem
of his own fluency. To any serious reader of modern theology, anyone who has wrestled first-hand with the texts of
Bonhoeffer, Bultmann, and most especially of Paul Tillich,
Robinson's shorthand appropriation of their most complex
ideas would have appeared, at least by comparison, to be facile.
He employs their ideas as if they were household currency,

when in fact neither clergy nor laity were generally well acquainted with them. While there certainly was serious theological work in the England of the 1960s, much of that work remained safely out of the hands of the parish clergy, and the theological college curricula of the day were largely confined to fitting candidates for ordination and parochial work. Only the universities, and not always they, were generally interested in what Robinson called the 'teutonic sources' of serious theological discourse, and it is perhaps not outrageous to suggest that Tillich, Bultmann and Bonhoeffer enjoyed wider credibility in American theological faculties than they did in British.

Those in the know would argue, with only that sort of condescension characteristic of the expert, that little, if anything, in *Honest to God* was new or novel. The professionals would accuse the bishop of being an amateur, but the fact remains that while his issues had been the stuff of professional debate for at least half a century, that 'stuff' had never reached the pews: it was theological shop-talk, a discourse among the cognoscenti. Not since Bishop Colenso, with the possible exception of Bishop Barnes, did an English bishop capture the public's theological imagination; and what to many seemed to hint of heresy in Robinson's book had been a part of professional debate for at least 50 years. For many of the devoutly ignorant, however, this was both new news and bad news. For many, Robinson was their introduction to the twentieth century world of secular existentialism, and, in the words of one of Paul Tillich's most famous sermons, it amounted to a 'shaking of the foundations'.

Perhaps at no place did Robinson's work cut closer to the bone than in the realm of ethics, or in what he called the 'new morality'. People may confess to knowing nothing of theology, and they may not even be 'religious' in the sense of the knowledgeable performance of duties, but everybody has a sense of what morals are and, for many, religion and morals are the same thing. Robinson argues that Christianity is identified with the old traditional morality, which would be acceptable, he argues, if the old morality were identifiably Christian. It is not, however, and for Robinson this was a problem, because in the tide that sweeps away morality as a creature of culture and not of faith, the faith so intimately identified with it might be swept away as well. Were he to extend Bultmann's distinction between *kerygma* and *mythos*, where the essential truth must be distinguished from the cultural *mythos* or context in which it is expressed, Robinson would say that morals themselves are constructed out of the materials of the age, whereas the faith transcends the age and should not be confused with it. If morals and the faith are the same, or morals are an indissoluble expression of the faith, then when the moral consensus breaks down and evolves into something else, the faith is likely to suffer the consequences.

Writing in England in 1963, within the recent memory of the *Lady Chatterley* obscenity case, Robinson would have found himself in the middle of what even the most obtuse layperson would recognize as a revolution in morals. That was the age in which the older generation would have remembered the rectitude of George V and Queen Mary, the scandal of the abdication of Edward VIII brought about by the vexed subject of divorce and adultery, and the disavowal of a romance of Princess Margaret on the grounds that the man in question was divorced and the Church of England would disapprove. That old standard was openly flouted by the generation of 'Angry Young Men' whose social revolution was staged to the music of the Beatles and costumed by the self-indulgent excesses of Carnaby Street; and if a clearly smutty book like *Lady Chatterley's Lover* could be found not to be obscene, then the moral ground was shifting under the very feet of the culture. The traditional response was a call to a revival of religion, but the problem was that the old religious sanctions – shame and damnation – were no longer seen to be working. If religion was to survive the inevitable secular transformation

it would have to be disentangled from the traditional morality, and as this 'new morality' was recognized by Pius XII as a
threat to established religious conviction, he denounced it on
18 April 1953. Four years later, the Holy Office condemned
the effort to deal with this phenomenon of situational or
existential ethics, and forbade the discussion of these theories
among Catholic moralists.

Robinson, not wanting to become an ethical Dame
Partington, who tried to sweep back the waters of the incom-
ing tide with her broom, embraced yet another theologian
of modernity, Joseph Fletcher of the Episcopal Theological
School in Cambridge, Massachusetts. 'Situational Ethics'
was not simply doing as you please or making it up as you
go along, although Joe Fletcher had many critics in America
who accused him of advocating this position. He was not.
Robinson understood that the correct behaviour in a situation was to be determined not by some settled law but by
the principle that 'compassion for persons overrides the law'.
He cites Matthew 12.3, where David appropriates the 'bread
of Presence', reserved for the priests, to feed himself and his
hungry men, and his action is approved, not condemned, by
Jesus. Robinson calls this a 'dangerous' ethic, likely to invite
the scrupulous attention of the legal Pharisees, and for that
reason people might fear it. 'Yet,' says Robinson, 'I believe it is
the only ethic for "man come of age." To resist it in the name
of religious sanctions will not stop it: it will only ensure that
the form it takes will be anti-Christian.'[2]

Robinson applies his 'dangerous' ethic to the vexed subject
of divorce, the hot-button moral issue of the day. Everybody
knew something about divorce; a king gave up his throne
because of it and social sanctions were exercised because of it,
and on this subject both the Roman Catholics and the Anglicans
were largely agreed: they were against it. Based upon tradition
and scripture, the Church's sanctions against divorce seemed
to be the one absolute left in a sea of relativity. For Robinson

to introduce divorce as the test case for a situation that would divorce religion from certain cultural norms was to invite trouble. It was possible, on the situational principle, to argue that in certain cases marriage was bad and divorce was good, the principle being that compassion for the individual overrides the law.

The debate on divorce, and Robinson's embrace of situationalism, a foreshortened discussion of which occurs in his chapter on 'The New Morality', tends to overshadow the broader but quite specific ethical principle that he earlier introduced as the basis of Christian behaviour and belief. If we believe that to be a Christian is to claim to know and to follow the mind of Christ, then our behaviour, our conduct as Christians, will proceed from what we understand that mind to be. Thus, the only absolute is Christ's love. Robinson is quite clear when he says:

> This is what it means for the Christian to 'have the mind of Christ,' to let his actions be governed, as Jesus enjoined, simply and solely by the love with which 'I have loved you,' or, in St. Paul's words, to 'let your bearing towards one another arise out of your life in Christ Jesus.
>
> Life in Christ Jesus, in the new being, in the Spirit, means *having no absolutes but his love, being totally uncommitted in every other respect but totally committed in this.*[3]

This is what is called an 'ethic of love'. Employing Paul Tillich's notion that 'Love alone can transform itself according to the concrete demands of every individual and social situation without losing its eternity and dignity and unconditional validity', the ethic of love, according to Robinson, is prepared to see every moment as a fresh creation from God's hand demanding its own and perhaps wholly unprecedented response.[4] This is nothing less than Tillich's ethics of the *Kairos*: 'Ethics in a changing world must be understood as the ethics of the *kairos* – of the God-given moment, mediating the meeting with the eternal in the temporal.'[5]

Tillich had expressed these views in *The Protestant Era*, which he had written in 1948, the same year in which his first volumes of sermons, *The Shaking of the Foundations*, was published; both Tillich and Fletcher were names well known in theological circles. The ethic of love as the sole absolute, and its situational application under the rubric of compassion, formed the basis of an entirely new response of Christian faith to an evolving social circumstance, one in which traditional morality, heretofore twinned with Christianity, was now to be evaluated in terms of the 'new' morality, which in fact was as old as Jesus and Paul.

Robinson recognized the controversial nature of this 'new' ethic. He knew that, for all of the best reasons, the moral guardians would at first be suspicious, then they would object, and ultimately they would resist. This was part of the danger of the 'dangerous ethic'. He was not naïve on this point, but this knowledge did little to inhibit what more cautious writers would call his 'incendiary phrases'. Love is the end of the law, because it has an unconditional respect for persons. Because it is absolute, love has the power to 'go into the concrete situation to discover what is demanded by the predicament of the concrete to which it turns'. Neither Roman Catholics nor evangelicals could take much comfort in this, addicted as they are to absolutes and standards, and in case they were uncertain as to what he meant, Robinson makes it clear: 'for persons are more important even than "standards"'.[6]

To the charge of relativism, Robinson says that the answer is not a 'recall to religion', which is the only recourse that the conventional church believes that it has. To reassert the 'sanctions of the supernatural', is to reinvest in a world-view already proven bankrupt. The claims of the new morality are those found among those who search even where God is not to be found, who look for meaning in the absence of supernaturalism and irrationality. His paradigm here is the post-Easter experience of the Emmaus Road in Luke 24:

> It is to join those on the Emmaus Road who have no religion left, and there, in, with and under the meeting of man with man and the breaking of our common bread, to encounter the unconditional as the Christ of our lives.[7]

In rereading *Honest to God* after 40 years, I continue to be profoundly grateful, and even moved, by the courage it took to write such a book. This was not, however, so much a calculated courage as it was inadvertent. Certainly, Robinson knew that he would create something of a furore by putting these views before the public. The *Chatterley* affair had given him the exposure to, if not the taste for, controversy; and if he had been just another Cambridge don writing on the speculative edges of orthodoxy, he would probably have remained in academic obscurity, and, as a result, presumably would have gained some modest preferment in a church that in modern times likes its bishops very tame. In two cases, however, he overestimated the capacity of his audience, or, as we would say today, his market.

First, I think he did not realize the extent of the theological illiteracy of the general populace. Obviously, by 1963, with a few uninterrupted weeks in which to think and write, he could take the benefit of nearly 20 years of deep and wide theological reading that addressed the existential dilemma in which he believed he was living. For the nineteenth century it was modern science, with Darwin in particular, that had brought the crisis of belief forward into what was to be called modernity. For Paul Tillich, it was the crisis of World War One; and for Bonhoeffer, the Nazi terror of World War Two. How modern man could continue to believe in meaning, when science, technology and the existential dilemma compromised the very notion of meaning in any traditional sense, was the agenda for the theologically thoughtful in the first half of the

century. For some, the response was the appeal of orthodoxy
and fundamentalism; for others it was existential despair; and
for people like Robinson it was the effort to recast a faith that
made sense for 'man come of age'.

Second, what made him annoying to so many of his critics
was his steadfast identification of himself as a churchman, one
who was not going to go away or give up his inheritance. Had
he declared no hope, or, in the style of Albert Camus, 'No
Exit', and then left the Church, people might have both for-
given and forgotten him. The fact that he claimed a Christian
solution compatible with the gospel, if not with the culture,
exasperated those who felt that the luxury of his honesty
was putting the whole household of faith at risk in a world
that was prepared to either ignore it or destroy it. He did not
understand that his audience could not go readily where he
would take them, for the simple reason that they were by no
means yet where he was.

What he could not have imagined in 1963 would be the
state of Christian behaviour and belief 40 years on, and for
this we cannot condemn him, as he made no pretensions to
prophecy. How could he have guessed that the philosophical questions that drove the theological debates of the first
half of the twentieth century would be resolved for many by
an aggressive appeal to a pre-critical reality? Harry Emerson
Fosdick assumed that the answer was a resounding 'no', as
he preached in his famous sermon, 'Shall the Fundamentalists Win?' in New York City in the early 1920s, and that a
system indifferent to the existential dilemmas of modern 'man
come of age' would collapse of its own weight. How wrong
he was. The world to which Robinson addressed his book,
and which responded with such convulsions, is no longer the
same world.

Liberal angst has been outmanoeuvred by the kinds of
religion that would be interested neither in Robinson's
problems nor his solutions. The only theological debate that

roils the church of which he was once bishop is the topic of homosexuality, argued implacably from traditional morality based upon a pre-critical reading of Scripture designed to sustain the status quo and based upon prejudices grounded in culture and not in gospel. The theologians – and the theologies – who nourished him continue to remain outside the pale of popular religious enthusiasm. One thing that would perhaps surprise Robinson is that 40 years after *Honest to God*, belief is no longer in retreat. The nature of the belief that now so widely prevails would perhaps disappoint him, however, and the ethic of life, where persons are more important than standards, remains as dangerous now as it was when Robinson decided to be honest in its espousal 40 years ago. The danger of a subversive ethic such as this provokes the religious to avoid it in order to save the faith, and the irony remains that that faith may very well yet be destroyed by those who fight to save it, because they are unwilling to risk the Church for the absolute and unconditional love of Christ.

Some argue that *Honest to God* asks and answers questions in which not many people are any longer interested, and some will argue that John Robinson was too facile in his efforts at honesty and, as a result, made things more rather than less complicated. These things may be, although I cannot recall another book of theology, popular or otherwise, published 40 years ago that still has the capacity to provoke and stimulate. Archbishop Rowan Williams describes Robinson's chapter on ethics as among his weakest: I could not disagree more. I would call it his most dangerous because of the power of the dangerous ethic of absolute love to change things. It was the radical ethic of absolute love that challenged the status quo in a world in which such an ethic was alien; and the new commandment that Jesus gave to his disciples on the eve of his own death was the ethic of absolute love: 'A new commandment I give to you, that you love one another; even as I have loved you, that you also love one another' (John 13.34; RSV).

This principle of persons is regarded as superior to all of the 'standards', and thus this ethical principle, to adapt once again Robinson's category, becomes a dangerous, even subversive, ethic. Such an ethic allowed Gandhi to triumph in his principle of non-violence; such an ethic empowered Martin Luther King, Jr., in his struggle against the powers and principalities; and such an ethic can be ascribed to the moral revolution that enabled the political revolution in South Africa under Nelson Mandela and Desmond Tutu.

To the charge of cultural relativism, which the orthodox were all too willing to level at any challenge to the absolute standards of revealed religion and the natural conservatism of cultural norms, Robinson responded with the appeal of the absolute of love as revealed in Jesus Christ and mediated with the situational norms to which both Tillich and Fletcher subscribed. For Robinson, in the new morality, the only way out of the moral morass of cultural relativism was by the claims of the absolute ethic of love as made real in Jesus and communicated in the frail flesh of human beings, 'for persons are more important than "standards"'. Nothing could be more clear.

Mark Twain once said that the things that troubled him about the Bible were not the things that he could not understand, but the things that were perfectly clear. He might have said the same of *Honest to God*.

NOTES

1 Trevor Beeson, *The Bishops*, SCM Press, 2003, p. 74.
2 Robinson, *Honest to God*, p. 117.
3 Robinson, *Honest to God*, p. 114, emphasis added.
4 Robinson, *Honest to God*, p. 115.
5 Robinson, *Honest to God*, p. 115.
6 Robinson, *Honest to God*, p. 120.
7 Robinson, *Honest to God*, p. 121.

6. Behaviour and Belief:

The Reduction of Religion to Ethics?

TREVOR HART

God and Goodness

The suggestion that religion and morality are inextricably entwined should come as no great surprise to anyone. Where they are held, beliefs about who God is, what God is like and how God is engaged with the world all function morally in the broad sense that (together with all sorts of other beliefs about what is the case) they will make a difference to the ways in which people live their lives. More specifically, of course, particular beliefs about divinely ordained and proscribed patterns of human behaviour may be central to some religious traditions, and commitment to a more or less closely defined moral pattern, therefore, part of the meaning of religious adherence itself.

Toward the end of the eighteenth century, the philosopher Immanuel Kant laid particularly heavy emphasis on this linkage between religion and morality, but at the same time he excluded God from the sphere of things about which humans could legitimately claim to 'know'. Kant's intention was not as such to deny the reality of God, but rather to insist that – if God had reality – it must by definition fall beyond the reach of human reason, and our claims about it must be of quite another sort than the 'scientific' statements we confidently make about states of affairs confronting us in the world. Hence his famous claim that he was limiting the scope of reason in order to 'make room for faith'. In fact, Kant suggested, 'belief' in God seems finally to be necessary in one way or another in order to undergird human ethical convictions and endeavour, which otherwise (since they too fall beyond the reach of rational demonstration) appear rather arbitrary.

Kant's voice has perhaps exercised an undue influence upon theological as well as philosophical thinking in the past two centuries or so. Certainly, this same combination of acknowledging the moral force of religious beliefs while placing scare quotes around the statements religious believers make about God (so as to mark them off decisively from other sorts of statements as having a peculiarly problematic status) has cropped up again and again in different forms. The efforts of the so-called logical positivists in the early twentieth century to limit the 'meaningfulness' of human statements to the sphere of that which could be tested empirically (i.e., verified or falsified in terms of some observable difference in the state of affairs pertaining in the world)[1] put even greater pressure on religious believers, threateing now to drive their statements about God further from the centre of intelligent discourse into the shadowy realm of the meaningless. Well-intentioned responses to such claims, in seeking to justify and account for the continued use of God-talk, have sometimes secured its street credibility only at a considerable price, redescribing it in essentially 'non-cognitive' terms and in doing so seeming to turn it from talk about God into a different sort of talk altogether.

One version of this has involved a virtual collapsing of the meaning of religious statements down to the level of ethical ones. So, for example, in the 1950s R. B. Braithwaite argued that religious assertions could, *mutatis mutandis*, essentially be assimilated to ethical ones, and a religious believer's claim that God is good 'be taken to declare his intention to follow

an agapeistic way of life'.[2] Despite the fact that such revisionist philosophical accounts view talk about God in ways that
depart drastically from the ways in which it has been (and
continues to be) understood and used by the majority of religious people, they found echoes among theologians eager to
commend religion to a wider set of intellectual concerns.

It is out of this broad milieu that John Robinson's project
in *Honest to God*[3] needs to be interpreted. In Chapter 6 of the
book, Robinson reflects directly the impact of the post-Kantian
'double-whammy', calling into question the way statements
about God have traditionally been understood, while at the
same time acknowledging the deep moral significance of such
statements. His response, as we shall see, follows a path similar to that trodden by Braithwaite, linking statements ostensi-
bly 'about God' directly to statements about the moral reality
of love, and doing so in such a way as to at least leave wide
open the suggestion that these are simply two ways of talking
about the same thing.

Later in this essay I shall respond critically to this proposal,
and question the moral force of the alternative account of
Christian 'God-talk' that Robinson provides. First though, on
the basis of the above, I want to pose a clarificatory question
about his wider project in *Honest to God*. What precisely is
Robinson asking us to recognize or believe about the status
of traditional Christian symbols (language, images) for God?
There are, it seems to me, at least two possibilities. Is he 1.
asking us to recognize that the reality we refer to through
such symbols is not as such a person (or even persons) who
has called the world into being, who dwells 'in the heavens'
rather than 'on earth', who loves and cares for and interacts
with what he has made, and who calls and seeks to draw us
together with his whole creation toward a promised future in
which our character will conform more perfectly to his own.
In other words, we might say, God is not 'in himself' the way
that the Bible and Christian tradition typically pictures and

speaks of him.[4] Is this the main burden of Robinson's case, to get us to acknowledge that 'in reality', as we might say, God is not as the Christian imagination has pictured him, is not 'really like' that at all? Or 2. is Robinson going further, and suggesting that the Christian imaging of God (the character-istic 'symbolic' structure of Christian faith as we might say) is unhelpful, intellectually unrespectable, perhaps even morally dangerous,[5] and ought now to be set aside in preference for some alternative?

Irreducibly Poetic: Reckoning with the Theological Small Print

The first option may sound drastic at first hearing; but it isn't really. While it may provide a qualification that is religiously and theologically important for certain purposes, in itself it permits us mostly to continue using the traditional symbols with impunity, and can safely be left buried in the 'small print' so far as our everyday faith and practice is concerned. It is, in fact, hardly a radical or new insight, but something that the mainstream of Christian theology has always recognized, and that must itself, ironically, be said to rest on profoundly bibli-cal insights about God's otherness with respect to the world. 'My thoughts are not as your thoughts, nor are your ways my ways,' says the Lord through Isaiah (55.8); and the biblical depiction of God as a whole, cast as it is and must inevitably be in images borrowed from this world, nonetheless betrays a deep awareness of the fragility and inadequacy of its own language where talk of the God who is not 'of' this world is concerned. It recognizes, we might say, that there is an inher-ently 'poetic' quality to all such language, since here old words are being taught new tricks, conscripted into a service for which they were not initially intended. And when the fourth-century theologian Athanasius insists that we cannot properly say of God that he 'exists' because 'existence' is something that pertains to creatures, he acknowledges the same truth, and in doing so presages something, at least, of Robinson's own insistence. He recognizes, that is to say, that this-worldly categories do not properly apply to God who is not 'like' any creaturely thing at all, but the radically different uncreated source of all the things to which our words are designed to apply. But Athanasius, while laying down this qualification, was nonetheless perfectly happy to go on to think and speak at great length of God in terms of the biblical symbols and developments of them. Why?

First, because like his biblical predecessors he realized that silence was not an option for Christian faith. Faith, whatever else it was, was about having heard and received, and in turn handing on, something said. The phenomenon of 'faith', we might say, can neither exist nor be nurtured apart from some shared symbolizing of its object, some way of picturing and speaking of God that captures and shapes our imagination, and directs our dispositions ('heart', mind, will and so on) and actions with respect to God, the world and other people. Creaturely symbols are, of course, the only currency we have to use in this process of transmission and transformation. Recognition that they are applied to God only by borrowing them from their mundane settings and 'teaching them new tricks' need not in and of itself lead us either to abandon them or seek to exchange them for some other set, if we suppose we have good reason to suppose some particular set helpful – and perhaps for supposing it to be more appropriate than other possible ways of imagining how things lie between God and the world. And this, no doubt, would be Athanasius's second point. Christians traditionally have supposed precisely this. Their claim that the God whose reality lies beyond the ordinary reaches of human thought and speech has 'made himself known' (itself, of course, an irreducibly and unashamedly anthropomorphic and poetic way of speaking, drawn from the sphere of human relationships) is in effect the claim that

God has endorsed the use of certain words and pictures and stories (a particular poetics) in terms of which to think and speak of him. It is, in more familiar parlance, the claim that God has himself 'spoken', and in doing so has provided both a basis and a guideline for the shape of our responsive speech to and about him. It is precisely because of, and not despite the point which Kant so helpfully emphasizes – that God does not belong to this world and that the conditions for knowledge and speech about God do not therefore ordinarily exist – that Christian theology is finally driven back to this remarkable claim, and must either take it seriously or else concede that all speech about God is generated merely by the engines of human religious invention. If God can be known and spoken of appropriately, then it is only because God has accommodated himself to our weakness, has straddled the yawning gap (uncrossable from our side) between his own reality and the sphere of the creaturely, and given himself to be known and spoken of. The shape of this self-accommodation, though, is – precisely because it must be – thoroughly poetic.

'How shall we think of the kingdom of God?' asks Jesus; and his answer takes the form of an appeal to a series of familiar images in terms of which the transcendent and unfamiliar reality may helpfully be pictured: 'think of it as if it were an expensive pearl, a great banquet, a mustard seed' and so on. Each image falls woefully short, of course, of capturing the reality of the kingdom of God, because the kingdom is in fact literally none of these things. But each image may nonetheless convey something very important about the kingdom through a certain appropriate analogy between them. As theologian Sallie McFague reminds us in her helpful study of the role of metaphor in religious and theological language, metaphorical statements 'always contain the whisper, "it is and it is not"'.[6] There is both likeness and unlikeness (and perhaps a considerable amount of the latter) posited between two realities when metaphor is used. The kingdom of God cannot be mounted in a necklace, gatecrashed or cultivated on damp blotting paper.

It may be argued that God's self-revealing as a whole, and not just elements in Jesus' teaching, is properly 'parabolic' in nature, and that Christian talk about this God is inherently metaphorical. The unique 'otherness' which Christians believe characterizes God's reality relative to the world God has made makes it necessary to suppose so. After all, such a God can no more 'literally' be a father, a king, a shepherd, or a judge than we suppose the kingdom of God actually to be a pearl of great price, or a banquet, or a mustard seed. To suggest otherwise would be to miss the truth about God's all-surpassing greatness, to belittle God by confusing him with some part of his creation. But God grants us this series of images (and many others), drawn from the familiar world of human experience, in terms of which to think and speak about and to him. Were God not to do so we should have only two options: agnostic silence or speculative invention. Faith trusts that these divinely furnished images are indeed appropriate rather than inappropriate ones, giving us a fitting poetic handhold on God's own reality. But faith also recognizes that this same reality nonetheless eludes capture and definition under any set of human terms. Christian faith is thus irreducibly poetic. Even though we know that God's reality transcends all creaturely realities, and that we must therefore acknowledge in the small print of our faith that God is not literally a Father, not literally a maker of things, not literally located 'out there' and so on, nonetheless, on the basis of God's own self-unfolding (another metaphor!) we venture to 'see God as'[7] one of whom such things are appropriately said, and live and speak for most purposes as those who take such things as 'true', in the same way that we take it to be true that light is constituted in the form of waves – or should that be particles?

'It is, and it is not.' Acknowledgement of the 'and it is not' may be something we should call to mind from time to time

in order to avoid idolatry and a concomitant loss of sense of
wonder and awe in God's presence. But to seek to live in the
light of such small print from moment to waking moment is
quite unnecessary, and would in fact constitute something
approaching religious neurosis. We do not, after all, perform
such mental gymnastics in other directly analogous cases.
Most people in our society 'know' in some important but
nonetheless detached way that the sun does not 'really' rise
or set, that it is we rather than it who are moving through
space at an incredible velocity, that the ground beneath our
feet – which feels so solid and secure – is actually the surface
of a spinning ball from which we are prevented from hurtling
into space only by an invisible force called gravity. We 'know'
these and many other potentially worrying things because
science reads us the small print disclaimers in the contract of
life on earth. But we do not live our lives from moment to
moment in the nail-biting awareness of them. To do so would
be odd indeed, and we are perfectly content to keep them in
the background while we get on with our lives in the relatively
stable world that presents itself to us. We should only attempt
some wholesale un-imagining and re-imagining of things if we
were convinced that the received version were intellectually
dishonest, detrimental in some way to our well-being and that
of others, and could (and therefore should) be exchanged for
something better.

We may and must acknowledge the inherent and irreduc-
ible 'poetry' of Christian talk about God, therefore, without
capitulating in any way to suggestions either that such talk is
'non-cognitive', or that its ultimate source lies hidden in the
creative genius of humankind. To argue in such ways seriously
misunderstands the cognitive status of certain sorts of imaginative activity and grants far too much credit to a Romantic
view of poetry. It also fails to see how certain claims which
Christians make about God and God's relation to the world
logically involve acknowledgment that when God appropri-

ates creaturely form in acts of self-revelation we are presented with a cosmic trope.

Motives for Re-imagining?

Honest to God seems to me to prevaricate unhelpfully on the question of what to do about the theological small print. There seems to be a tension in the author's thought that remains unresolved throughout the book.

Robinson does seem to indicate fairly clearly that for considerations of an apologetic sort as well as ones connected with intellectual integrity, the old symbols really should now be set aside as inherently unhelpful and well past their use-by date. Being 'honest' to God at all seems at first glance to involve no less than ceasing to pretend, suspending the imaginative suspension of disbelief that faith involves, refusing the 'as if', the imagined world that the traditional symbols offer, and embracing in its stead something else more honest, clear-headed and helpful. The mental picture of the God-world relation that the traditional symbolism provides may now, Robinson suggests, be more of a stumbling block than an aid to belief in the gospel. As we shall see, Robinson also offers a measured critique of 'the old, traditional morality'[8] and its connection with the 'supranaturalist way of thinking' in religion, and again construes it as unhelpful for reasons that have to do with more than mere apologetics. Surely, if even this much is true, then revision, redescription is precisely what is called for, for the sake of those inside as well as those outside the Church, and the sooner the better?

On the other hand, though, there are persistent suggestions in *Honest to God* that there is nothing inherently wrong with the traditional 'poetics of Christian faith' at all, that (despite the recognition that in the poetry of faith more than any other the 'it is' must be balanced by the 'it is not') the images around which the tradition is structured may actually play a vital continuing role in daily faith and practice; and not just for the naïve, but for those who have read the small print and survived. Perhaps for apologetic purposes we may need to consider whether traditional images may constitute a barrier rather than a bridge. But among the faithful, Robinson suggests, such images might have a significant and perhaps even an indispensable role to perform. So, for example, he writes even at the very end of his book, 'it may be impossible to imagine the personal ground of all our being except as an almighty Individual, endowed with a centre of consciousness and will like ourselves, and yet wholly "other". As symbols', he continues, 'these images have their powerful and their proper place. They . . . become dangerous only when they cease to mediate the reality and indeed become barriers to it.'[9] With this, it seems to me, no representative of the theological mainstream could reasonably disagree, and for reasons that, as noted above, have nothing to do with abandoning the shape of the tradition, but precisely because of things which that tradition itself compels us to suppose about God, a God to whose reality it refers us in images borrowed from this world but who is pictured precisely as refusing to be contained by or confused with any of them.

The passage just cited may, though, betray another inconsistency in Robinson's case to which attention should be drawn. The suggestion that, in trying to imagine the ground of our being, we inevitably end up using personal images such as those furnished by the tradition, seems to presume that 'the ground of our being' itself is a more absolute conception that lies somewhat abstractly and obscurely behind such attempts to imagine it. Robinson sometimes privileges his revisionist account of God, speaking of it as though it succeeds in short-circuiting the need for imagination, vision or parable, and cut through to the 'demythologized' reality of the matter. This, of course, is not so, as Robinson at his best readily recognizes. To speak of God as 'the ground of our being' is not an unimaginative or direct accounting of God's reality enjoying something like 'scientific' warrant, but simply an alternative way of imagining the reality of God, drawing just as surely upon this-worldly categories as does the tradition. We can no more say that God 'is' the ground of our being than we can say that God exists, or is a Father, or loves us, without immediately conceding that the words 'is' and 'ground' and 'Being' are used here parabolically. It's not that God is really like this, rather than really like the traditional imagery. Rather this is offered to us as an alternative picture of how things stand, an imaginative redescription set within an alternative vision of God's relatedness to the world. So we have two poetic (as opposed to one poetic and one more 'scientific') offerings on the table. And we are invited to consider the respective merits of each.

At this juncture one might say a good deal (though here a little must suffice!) about the sort and the levels of freedom that Christians may legitimately exercise with respect to the received imaginative heritage of the Church. I have suggested above that the mainstream has been committed to the view that God has provided, as it were, a reservoir of images and stories in terms of which to think and speak about and to him, laying hold of the human imagination and shaping it in particular ways, fitting it most appropriately to apprehend his own mysterious and supramundane reality. If one takes this claim about God's self-revealing initiative seriously (and doing so seems to me to be intrinsic to the status which the Church attaches to the Bible's authority as 'Scripture'), one need not limit Christian God-talk to the rehearsal of this particular set of imaginative resources, but one will certainly want to grant them some sort of normative or controlling influence on whatever developments in theology and liturgy are undertaken. Issues about the adjustment of language to shifting cultural contexts will then take the form of serious considerations of the continuity and discontinuity of particular trajectories of development, about their 'faithfulness' to (as effectively improvised extensions of) the basic pattern of that which has been received. Robinson, though, has little at all to say in his book about God's self-revealing, or about the responsibilities under which it might place those who undertake to modify the language of faith. Much of what he says seems to suppose that the development of a religious symbolics is an essentially proactive rather than a responsive activity of imagination, and that the task of the apologist or the theologian is to identify, adopt and develop those ways of thinking and speaking about God that most fully commend themselves to the wider populace. In what follows, therefore, rather than measuring Robinson's own poetic proposals against the shape of the story that the Church has told and tells about God and the world, we shall do so on purely pragmatic grounds. In comparing it to the more traditional version of things, we shall consider the likely impact of each on the shaping of the self as a moral entity.

Redescribing God and Relocating Moral Authority

Together with the received ways of thinking and speaking of God, Robinson eschews what he calls 'the old, traditional morality'.[10] This, he seems to suppose, is mostly a matter of passive obedience to a set of commands or laws laid down from above by God, and possessed of universal significance for human beings. Here, then, is a clear enough connection between belief and behaviour, but one which must now be discarded, because it is unworthy of a humanity come of age and mature enough to take responsibility for its own moral judgements. Indeed, for the Church to insist upon earthing its responses in such an approach courts apologetic disaster in a secular culture, since the reasons on which it is based ('God has decreed x a sin') 'have force, and even meaning, for none but a diminishing religious remnant'.[11] Yet the fundamental ethical questions 'Why shouldn't I?' or 'What's wrong with it?' remain ones pressing for an answer by 'secular' as well as 'religious' people. As we have noted, Robinson does not go as far as Richard Holloway's claim that traditional ways of imagining God's significance for human morality are inherently damaging, bound up organically with the commission of acts of moral harm (legitimating oppressive behaviour, encouraging an ethic based on fear, etc.); but the burden of his account nonetheless adds up to the dual claim that (1.) it would be better for the Church in apologetic terms and (2.) better for the course of human moral development more widely were such traditional views to be let go of. Nor, unlike Holloway, does he advocate cutting the tie between ethics and belief in God altogether, but rather re-imagines the nature of the relationship between them in the process of re-imagining the meaning of 'God-talk' itself. The outcomes, though, it might be suggested, are largely similar in practical terms because of the contours of the new 'religious poetics' that Robinson adopts.

In Robinson's version of things, the authorization of human actions is effectively cut free from anything resembling an appeal to God as the transcendent personal source of goodness and truth. For Robinson, God is now to be spoken and thought of in 'non-transcendent' terms as the 'ground of being', the 'depth of ordinariness', and try as one might it is frankly very difficult to appeal to such a thing for guidance or strength and in doing so distinguish clearly what one is doing from drawing upon one's own moral resources. If God is pictured as having no identifiable reality 'other than' or 'beyond' the reality of which human lives consist (whether some deep substratum of that reality, or the reality as a whole) then, since we cannot actually abandon spatial metaphor in our bids to make sense of things, we shall find it very difficult to disentangle God's reality imaginatively from our own, and to see what difference the introduction of God-talk finally makes to anything (i.e., what it can tell us that the 'secular' discourses of psychology, anthropology, sociology, etc. cannot). That is precisely why the 'traditional' accounts of God use the poetic language of 'up there' and 'down here', which Robinson rejects at the outset of his book; not because in some primitive way they suppose God to be physically present somewhere else and absent 'down here' ('Where can I flee from your presence?' asks the psalmist), but because such spatial metaphor, properly used and balanced by images of closeness and indwelling, provides a vital poetic means of securing the theological truth that God is not 'of' this world, is other than it, is its source and basis and hope, is unconstrained by its limitations and possibilities. For the biblical writers, indeed, God is so radically 'other' than the created world we know that he is able to be closer to us than we are to ourselves, to know us better than we know ourselves.

The notion of 'transcendence', therefore, does not, if defined in terms of and developed in accordance with biblical ways of thinking and speaking, amount to remoteness, aloofness, lack of involvement or concern. On the contrary, it is the otherness of God, which this term connotes, that alone makes sense of the sort of radical closeness to, and involvement and identification with, his people of which the Bible speaks. But transcendence is usefully (perhaps vitally) pictured in terms of spatial distinction and distance for certain purposes at least, because it is in such terms that we naturally symbolize that which is other than ourselves. It is also, of course, how we most naturally picture the relationship to us of other persons, and therefore a natural expression of faith in a God who relates to us as persons do. In the light of this, Robinson's concession that in order to imagine the ground of our being adequately we may finally have to resort to something very like the traditional symbols is very telling.

As an alternative, Robinson offers us an imaginative redescription of the God–world relation that deliberately eschews 'the projection of supranaturalism',[12] and seeks to rehabilitate God-talk as a vital way of speaking about the numinous, mysterious depth of this world and our existence in it. Theological statements are 'an analysis of the depths . . . of all experience "interpreted by love"'[13] rather than 'descriptions' of 'a supreme Person, a self-existent subject of infinite goodness and power, who enters into a relationship with us comparable with that of one human personality with another'.[14] To say that 'God is personal' is thus not to posit such a 'person' at all, but 'to say that "reality at its very deepest level is personal", that personality is of ultimate significance in the constitution of the universe, that in personal relationships we touch the final meaning of existence as nowhere else'.[15] And so on. The grammar of this immanentist poetic risks a reduction of 'God's' involvement in human affairs to an aspect or dimension of the human world itself, capable of being described and accounted for in other, thoroughly this-worldly terms. Robinson desperately seeks to avoid such a reduction, and to preserve a discrete space for properly religious symbolism: 'There are depths of revelation, intimations of eternity, judgments of the holy and the sacred, awarenesses of the unconditional, the numinous and the ecstatic, which cannot be explained in purely naturalistic categories without being reduced to something else.'[16]

But 'naturalism' of the sort that Robinson envisages, with its reduction of everything to crude material components, has no monopoly on what I have referred to as the 'this-worldly'. It has been an unfortunate habit of Western theology often to draw lines of demarcation between the 'material' and the 'spiritual', the 'natural' and the 'supernatural', and then to run these lines closely together with that drawn between the reality of the world and the reality of God in such a way as to make confusion between them all too easily. The Eastern tradition has a clearer mind on the matter, insisting that the vital distinction falls between the 'uncreated' (God) and the 'created' (all that is not God). The latter category includes all sorts of 'spiritual' and 'supernatural' realities of course. In the Nicene Creed's preferred phrase, that which God has made embraces both 'things visible and invisible'. That the world and our existence in it manifests depth, mystery and intimations of numinousness; that our own humanity refuses to be reduced to the dimensions of a flesh and blood machine, but finds 'spirit', sacrality, ultimacy and a propensity to the ecstatic constantly bubbling up to the surface and craving expression, all of this is no doubt true and vitally important, and should not surprise us. It is, in the decades since *Honest to God* was first published, precisely what the so-called New Age religious movements and the burgeoning market in volumes on 'self and spirituality' have rediscovered. To talk about the spiritual and sacral depths of the creaturely, though, is not at all the same thing as talking about the God who calls the creaturely into existence, holds it from moment to moment in existence, and draws it lovingly towards its creaturely end. The question remains, therefore, whether, despite his best intentions, the 'reinterpretation' of God's transcendence that Robinson claims as his goal[17] really succeeds, or whether a way of speaking that recognizes the vital 'otherness' of God with respect to the creaturely has not effectively been bargained away for one which constantly sounds as though it were talking about creaturely realities, albeit deep and ultimate ones.

Reducing Religion to Ethics

This problem is nowhere more apparent than in Robinson's account of the 'new morality', which he proposes as a necessary correlate to his revised imagining of God. Robinson accounts for God-talk in the ethical context in terms of the vital difference made by our human perception of a given circumstance in the light of 'love'. Belief and behaviour, he insists, are inseparable precisely because 'assertions about God are in the last analysis assertions about Love – about the ultimate ground and meaning of personal relationships'.[18]

It is here, if anywhere, that the apparent reduction of religion to ethics in Robinson's thought takes place. Few Christians would want to deny that God is the ultimate ground and meaning of personal relationships, but they would not be happy simply to reverse the formula as if talk about love (or even Love) were what talk about God, in the final analysis, adds up to. It is considerably more than that, and the vital surplus makes all the difference to the way one understands 'love' and its place in our existence at all, and where one might be willing to recognize it. This interpretative 'framing' of the ethical circumstance includes its juxtaposition within a story about a personal God who, out of love, acts in certain radical ways in history and thereby shows us the true nature of love and furnishes a standard by which to measure our human approximations to it. Shorn of this 'mythological' background, Robinson's account is altogether more streamlined. With no divinely prescribed legislation to constrain it, and no mythological moral personality to model itself upon or correspond to in its actions and responses, Christian morality (and human morality more widely) must now operate on the basis of its own discernment of what constitutes 'love' in each particular circumstance. Such discernment is, of course, what true religion is all about, since 'Love' is what, in the final analysis, we are talking about when we speak of the reality of God. To discern God in a situation, and to identify the demands of love in that same situation are one and same thing. Nothing other than the demands of love are relevant in morality, since 'nothing else makes a thing right or wrong'.[19] Clearly this places a huge responsibility upon us in our task of moral discernment, but 'love . . . has a built-in moral compass, enabling it to "home" intuitively upon the deepest need of the other'.[20]

It is difficult to imagine a more confident ascription of the essential 'unity' between God and humanity than this. We are all at least capable of discerning intuitively what it is that 'God' demands of us in a situation, though the claim is rendered less breathtaking once we remind ourselves that 'what God demands' and 'what our deepest moral sensibility tells us' really amount to the same thing in the final analysis, and no metaphysical claim is being made. In Christian terms, there would appear here to have been a very significant loss of the sense that God stands over against us and judges us, finds us wanting, and must transform us before we become those whose spiritual sensibilities are 'naturally' attuned to his own. But once God's 'otherness' has been traded together with the mythological paraphernalia of 'commandments' and stories of morally relevant divine action, such a clear sense of moral 'otherness' becomes difficult to sustain. Henceforth, any moral imperative pressing for our attention will either be assimilated by definition as a function of our own highest moral insight or else dismissed on the basis that our moral compass does not register it as pointing us in the right direction. In either case it is we who appear to be making the relevant judgement for ourselves.

Immanentalism and the Risk of Moral Impotence

In his book *Sources of the Self*[21] philosopher Charles Taylor traces the deep connection between 'religiously' earthed imaginative visions of the good (of which the tradition, as we have noted, offers us one and Robinson another), and the shaping of human moral agency. To be human, Taylor contends, is to be faced by a constant barrage of behavioural choices, and in situating ourselves morally we refer tacitly to some overall imaginative 'take' on or description of the way the world is, of what is worth doing, of what sort of person it is good to be and become with respect to others and the world in which we find ourselves. Some such vision, Taylor insists, underwrites all human moral reflection and action, whether we are aware of it or not, and providing such a vision is one role

that religious faith (Christian or of other sorts) has traditionally performed for human societies. In *An Intelligent Person's
Guide to Modern Culture* [22] Roger Scruton concurs with this
judgement, and suggests that one of the dilemmas of modern
secularism has been its effective orphaning by the deliberate
abandonment of such frameworks, and its attempt to unearth
meaning and value in the finite itself. This Scruton suggests, is
finally a lost cause. Ethical vision, if it is to be something we
can live by, infusing our lives with value, turns out to need
some sort of genuinely transcendent referent. Genuinely secular ethics, he contends, all too easily collapses in on itself,
unable to lift itself off the ground by tugging at its own shoe-
laces. And the best thing for secular societies, he argues, would
actually be to live 'as if' God existed, 'as if' our lives mattered
on some eternal register of value, 'as if' we were creatures
held accountable by a higher judge than our own conscience
or social mores, and so on, even if intellectually we have long
since let go of any such beliefs.

Ethics, in other words, when analysed, seems to require some
imaginative, poetic vision of that which transcends the secular
to sustain it. This analysis, if it is in any way accurate, seems to
me somewhat ironic, given Robinson's suggestion that ethics,
mature ethics, ethics in a world come of age, should in effect
be conducted as if God did not exist, or at least as if the word
God did not mean most of the things which traditionally it has
for Christian faith. In other words, there is a serious question
as to whether, having deliberately shorn religion of a certain
sort of transcendence, one ends up discovering that one has
accidentally neutered its moral potency in the process.

In closing this essay I want, by way of a positive account of
how the traditional poetics of Christian belief has functioned
morally in certain respects, to defend it from some of the
charges Robinson lays at its door, and thereby to suggest its
relative merits in furnishing resources for moral transformation compared to his proposed alternative.

Rules, Responsibility and a Theology of Grace

First, perhaps, we should tackle head on the inference that the depiction of God as a transcendent, personal moral authority entails a command morality that is by definition unthinking and naïve in its responses. Of course the Christian tradition, like many others, deploys the language of divine commands to express the idea that God's own moral character has direct implications for the shape of human living. If God is indeed appropriately imagined as a moral personality whose reality impinges significantly upon human life, then at some point the impinging must become apparent in concrete rather than abstract terms, and in Scripture one way in which this occurs is through God actually telling people how they should and should not live in 'covenant' with him. The Ten Commandments and the Sermon on the Mount are two obvious central examples of such divine instruction. Robinson insists that appeal to such divinely sanctioned precepts (which he suggests for those who believe in them constitute absolutes about which there can be no doubt and which must simply be applied in every circumstance) lacks meaning for most enlightened people ('modern man' in his 1960s phrase) and should therefore be demythologized together with the picture of the Lawgiver. But this is both rather patronizing and a misrepresentation of the facts of the matter. Christians have always recognized that such 'commands' play only a partial role in the pursuit of the life of holiness. No matter how much is 'given' in this way, more will always be required than any simple or 'blind' obedience. No set of moral instructions could ever provide a complete map of the moral contingencies of human living. There will often be the need for interpretation, extrapolation, imaginative application of and improvization upon the basic framework or themes that such commands provide. Sometimes the challenges in this regard are quite significant, and the responses to them highly sophisticated and careful. The call to engage intelligently rather than unthinkingly with any source of moral authority is well taken. To denigrate any religious ethic entailing recognition of divine commands as exclusive of real moral responsibility or the exercise of freedom, though, is an unfortunate distortion of how such things work in reality.

To turn the matter around for a moment, one might add that it is far from clear that to be given less rather than more as a context for moral judgement and action (i.e., to have one's space for moral flexibility unconstrained by any transcendent moral authority) is the obvious pathway to liberation and responsible living, and something to be celebrated. The very opposite might be argued. The world as Robinson describes it, in which we are thrown back in every moral circumstance upon our own capacity as connoisseurs of 'love' will seem to many likely to be a threatening rather than a welcoming place. One of the distinct advantages of a rule-based ethic (whether religious or of some other sort) is precisely that it lifts a certain amount of pressure from the shoulders of the moral agent. No one can reasonably be expected to treat every fresh practical and moral context in daily living as an opportunity to prove his or her capacity for responsible consideration of all the relevant ins and outs and pros and cons of different moral responses to it. At some point we have actually to get on with living life! To have to make an original moral judgement in every new circumstance in life would be a fast track to a nervous breakdown, and we should quickly find ourselves paralysed by the overbearing sense of responsibility imposed upon us. If ever there were a recipe for fear, guilt and a sense of oppression then surely this would be it?

In practice, Christian believers, adherents of other religious traditions, and 'secular' inhabitants of modernity all indwell a moral cosmos messier and more complicated than the streamlined version that Robinson advocates as the hallmark of humanity come of age. We fall back on other considerations than our naked intuition, and in doing so we do not abandon moral responsibility, but exercise it. That is to say, we do what is needful in order to act morally, rather than standing and shivering in the face of the crushing demand to 'decide, decide, decide!' Sometimes we fall back tacitly on rules or 'commands' that are not meant in any way to prohibit moral responsibility, but to indicate what in most cases will almost certainly be the best thing to do, drawing at least on deep reservoirs of that wisdom generated by centuries of moral experience. 'Thou shalt not lie' does not rule out the likelihood that there will be cases where to lie is better than not to lie; but in 98 per cent of cases we can probably fall back on it as a good rule of thumb, and in terms of the development of moral character we would certainly be better advised to seek to become the sort of people who ordinarily do not lie than the sort who need to weigh the evidence and decide whether to lie or not whenever an opportunity for lying presents itself! Such rules may be God given, but secular cultures have their own codes of moral wisdom to perform an analogous function.

It is significant to note, then, that in Christian understanding, God's law arises within a context of grace. The Ten Commandments are given to Israel on Sinai, at the point where God has already chosen the people and delivered them from slavery, and now establishes the obligations of his covenant with them. 'I have chosen you,' God tells them, 'and you are going to be my people. Here's what that has to mean in practice.' So the law is an instrument of God's grace, and not an apparatus for securing divine favour by moral effort. It is meant precisely to lift the crushing burden of moral responsibility from human shoulders, to place limits on such responsibility without abrogating it altogether. Failure to 'keep' the law is certainly a serious matter because it posits an unbearable contradiction between the moral character of human existence and God's own moral nature; but within the wider patterns of Christian understanding such failure does not constitute an ultimate threat to our well-being under God, since God himself takes final responsibility for it in the atonement. Again, therefore, law and our keeping or failing to keep it must be set firmly within the context of God's gracious dealings with us. What Christians believe about God's redemptive action in Christ in fact sets us free to take the risk of moral living, by freeing us from the otherwise paralysing effect of guilt and fear of the consequences of failure. Divine rule-giving is important, but its significance will be seriously misunderstood if we abstract it from the broader texture of Christian faith and practice within which it properly belongs.

Redemption and the Reformation of Character

This leads us to a further significant observation about the way people live their lives morally, and the function of religious traditions (and God) in shaping such living. Rules are not the only, perhaps not even the primary factor additional to moral choosing. Very often we act morally without conscious reference to any rule or set of principles whatever. We act simply according to the sort of person we are and are becoming or, as we would say, according to our character. We act, that is to say, in accordance with moral habits that we have acquired, or moral virtues that have been inculcated in us. We act in ways that 'come naturally' to us to the extent that who we are is already a morally disposed (rather than a morally neutral) consideration. The formation and reformation of character, though, must be understood in context, and can be inculcated by the practice of certain of disciplines and the deliberate avoidance of particular behavioural patterns. More broadly and fundamentally, it will be inspired by some imaginative vision of what sort of person it is good to be, a vision that we may or may not be explicitly aware of at a given moral juncture, but that will profoundly influence the ways we act and the ways we feel about our actions, because it will shape our deepest moral responses to the world. For Christians, this vision of what it is good to be and to become humanly is bound up with – and cannot really be understood apart from – the story that faith has to tell about who God is, what God has done, and what God has promised. It is the imaginative 'indwelling' of this story as part of our own story that inspires, motivates and grants resources of hope for our engagements morally with the world. It is, of course, a story of sinfulness, forgiveness and redemption in the hands of a God whose words 'You shall be holy as I am holy' are heard as both demand and as promise. We are to strive to reflect God's own character in our daily living not in order to earn God's acceptance, but motivated by love and gratitude for the one who accepts us as we are and has committed himself to working in, with and through us by his Spirit until we begin to reflect more fully the pattern of a humanity made concrete in his Son. This humanity is anomalous in the world's terms, for, while we are called to 'perform it' in the midst of this world, it belongs finally to a promised new creation, which we are as yet able only to imagine and hope for. So, we are faced with an ethical paradox; we are called to live according to a pattern which, by definition and no fault of our own lies ever beyond us and cannot be realized fully in this world. Indeed, the attempt to realize it will almost certainly bring us into painful conflict with the world's standards and priorities. This is what Bonhoeffer called the 'cost of discipleship', and it is intrinsic to Christian identity.

Far from crushing us with impossible moral burdens, or reducing us to slaves of an alien and arbitrary justice, though, the widespread testimony of Christians across the centuries has been that the demanding pursuit of this same 'transcendent' humanity, within the context of God's gracious dealing with us in Christ, is one that brings liberation, delight and joy, as if we had 'come home' in moral terms for the first time. Ironically, from this standpoint it is sin, and not obedience, that binds and enslaves people to 'alien' patterns of life. Life lived in correspondence with God's own holiness enjoys the 'perfect freedom' of which the typically modern demand for moral autonomy knows and understands nothing.

This advocacy of the role of rules and habits/character is not meant in any way to deny the genuine need for careful moral judgements to be made in certain circumstances, circumstances in which to fail carefully to weigh the relevant factors and make an informed choice would be morally irresponsible. But most of our moral engagement is not like this and could not be. And we must reckon with the fact that those who engage in moral reflection and choice are particular people whose lives already have a heavy moral 'spin' on them. Such reflecting and choosing is never something done in a vacuum. Those who must choose and make judgements are real people with a history, an upbringing, a sense of what matters and what does not, even a sense of what does and does not constitute a moral question worthy of consideration. Habit, virtue, character and the subliminal impact of familiar moral codes cannot be erased from such contexts of choice. We cannot, in other words, become someone other than who we actually are in moral terms, and who we are makes a difference to what we are likely to choose and to do. (It will certainly have an impact, for example, on what we are capable of identifying as 'love'.)

Faith, Identity and the Limits of Religious Re-imagining

Christian faith (I do not presume to speak here for any other religious tradition, but something similar may well be true for others) is about a particular way of living in the world, which is to say that it is irreducibly moral. This certainly does not mean that such faith is a matter of simple subscription (let alone unthinking subscription!) to a set of moral maxims. As we have seen, while such rules have their place, they only have meaning and justification at all because of the wider context of 'beliefs' and practices within which they are set. More precisely, they make sense only within the framework of a particular

understanding of God, God's character and God's relationship to the world in which this character is unfolded. Christian
faith is about living in the world in the light of the knowledge
that its final purpose and meaning lies in the God whose identity is made known in the story told in Scripture. This story is
summarized by one recent text on ethics as follows:

> The God of Israel, the creator of the world, has acted
> [astoundingly] to rescue a lost and broken world through
> the death and resurrection of Jesus; the full scope of that
> rescue is not yet apparent, but God has created a community
> of witnesses to this good news, the church. While awaiting
> the grand conclusion of the story, the church, empowered
> by the Holy Spirit, is called to re-enact the loving obedience
> of Jesus Christ and thus to serve as a sign of God's redemp-
> tive purposes for the world.[23]

No doubt this summary could be tweaked or adjusted slightly.
But in its basic form it is a reliable synopsis of the storyline
of the book that Christians read in church day by day, and
that is unambiguously woven into the texture of its liturgies.
It is the story that Christians tell (to themselves and others)
and in accordance with which they seek to live life. To be
a Christian is to live in the world 'as' this world, to live in
obedient response to this God, to seek in all circumstances
to do nothing that cannot be offered to this God as an act of
service. It is to live in the light of what this God has done and
has promised to do. The identification and recognition of God
as a 'moral' personality, and the pursuit of a human way of
being in the world which corresponds to God's own moral
reality is thus not peripheral, nor even only desirable within
Christianity; it is what Christian faith is.

What all this suggests is that we cannot easily reconfigure
the pattern of Christian symbols in any drastic manner without
effectively abandoning what it has traditionally meant to be

and to live as a Christian at all. If we are urged to lay this particular imaginative vision aside, then we should certainly ask some searching questions about the moral and spiritual resources afforded by whatever is proposed in its place. The attenuated re-imagining of God which Robinson proposes, I suggest, were we to seek to live by it, to live in the world 'as' the world he depicts, would prove less rich and fruitful in moral terms than its traditional alternative and, were it to survive, within a generation or two would result in something unidentifiable as Christian faith at all. This was not, I think, what he either intended or hoped for. Perhaps, therefore, his expressed reluctance to deny outright the usefulness of the traditional symbols, and his recognition that, in some sense, imagining God as personal and even as father might actually be important to the shaping of a fruitful Christian piety, were rooted in weightier intuitions than he himself suspected when he wrote the book.

NOTES

1 See A. J. Ayer, *Language, Truth and Logic*, 2nd edn, Victor Gollancz, 1946, for a programmatic statement. For a helpful discussion of the issues see John Hick, *Philosophy of Religion*, Prentice-Hall, 1963, Chapter 7.
2 R. B. Braithwaite, 'An Empiricist's View of the Nature of Religious Belief', reprinted in John Hick (ed.), *Classical and Contemporary Readings in the Philosophy of Religion*, Prentice-Hall, 1964, p. 432.
3 In this essay all page references are to the new edition of the book in the SCM Classics series, SCM Press, 2001.
4 We should distinguish this from the sort of 'Spitting Image' caricature that, while it no doubt continues to populate the imaginations of too many people both within and without the Church, can easily be disentangled from the depiction of God in the tradition proper, and the loss of which is unlikely to disturb wider Christian sensibility. It is 'the tradition proper' that Robinson has in his sights.
5 That belief in God has been morally damaging has recently been proposed in no uncertain terms, for example, by the former Bishop

of Edinburgh, Richard Holloway, in his book *Godless Morality: Keeping Religion Out of Ethics*, Canongate, 1999. See the equally forthright response by Richard Bauckham in Chapter 4 of his *God and the Crisis of Freedom: Biblical and Contemporary Perspectives*, Westminster John Knox, 2002.

6 Sallie McFague, *Metaphorical Theology*, Fortress Press, 1982, p. 13.

7 Garrett Green refers to 'as' as 'the copula of imagination'. See *Imagining God: Theology and the Religious Imagination*, Harper & Row, 1989, especially Chapter 3.

8 Robinson, *Honest to God*, p. 73.

9 Robinson, *Honest to God*, p. 92.

10 Robinson, *Honest to God*, p. 73.

11 Robinson, *Honest to God*, p. 75.

12 Robinson, *Honest to God*, p. 34.

13 Robinson, *Honest to God*, p. 29.

14 Robinson, *Honest to God*, p. 28.

15 Robinson, *Honest to God*, p. 29.

16 Robinson, *Honest to God*, p. 33.

17 Robinson, *Honest to God*, p. 34.

18 Robinson, *Honest to God*, p. 72.

19 Robinson, *Honest to God*, p. 78.

20 Robinson, *Honest to God*, p. 79.

21 *Sources of the Self: The Making of the Modern Identity*, Cambridge University Press, 1989.

22 *An Intelligent Person's Guide to Modern Culture*, Duckworth, 1998.

23 Richard Hayes, *The Moral Vision of the New Testament*, HarperSanFrancisco, 1996, p. 193.

7. Jesus for Modern Man:

The Historical Significance of John Robinson's Christology

ALISTER MCGRATH

I write this article as one who did not know John Robinson personally. He is one of the many theologians I read in my working life, who I know only through their writings. My task as a theologian is to read such writers, partly because I wish to understand them, but partly because my own vision for theology entails the critical reappropriation of the past. In what ways can the ideas of past writers be taken, either in their original or adapted forms, and put to new life in the academy or church?[1] This approach is illustrated in works such as Jürgen Moltmann's *Crucified God*, which demonstrated the continuing utility and relevance of Martin Luther's theology of the cross to both church and academy.

In the past, I had read John Robinson's *Honest to God* while researching English Anglican theological trends of the 1960s, and had formed a generally negative impression of the work, partly in terms of its value to the Church, but chiefly in terms of its merits as an interpretation of the theology of Dietrich Bonhoeffer, Rudolf Bultmann and Paul Tillich. Like many others to have read the book, I came to the conclusion that Robinson's judgements were somewhat hasty and superficial, presumably reflecting the busy life of a bishop who did not have enough time to read and reflect with the depth such authors required.

The invitation to revisit the work was most welcome, especially as my focus would be different this time around. Instead of examining the work in general, I was to look at its Christology; instead of assessing the merits of Robinson's readings of Bonhoeffer, Bultmann and Tillich, I was to reflect primarily on its value for the Church a generation later. It was an attractive and interesting brief, and I gladly undertook it. The Church needs all the help it can get to speak the gospel meaningfully and powerfully to our culture. Robinson might well be a prophetic voice in such a context, allowing his misreadings of Bonhoeffer and others to be overlooked.

The Background

It has become a commonplace to speak of the 1960s as a time of turbulence, overwhelmed with a sense of weariness and exasperation at the settled convictions of the era. Political, social and religious debate was shaped by an unrelenting impatience with the ways of the past, a sense of ennui with existing ideas and values, and a strong belief that a new beginning lay just around the corner. The cultural mood of the period is caught well by Tom Wolfe in his essay 'The Great Relearning'.[2] It was all about sweeping everything aside, and starting all over again, 'following a Promethean and unprecedented start from zero'. To those who caught the vision, it was nothing less than entrancing, promising a bright and brave new world unfettered by the outdated constraints of their parents' generation.[3]

One immediate result of this development was that parents gradually came to see it as neither appropriate nor important to instruct their children in the Christian faith. In his major and well-researched study *The Death of Christian Britain*, Callum Brown argues persuasively that it was during the 1960s that the British churches went into a downward spiral 'to the margins of social significance'.[4] The loss of credibility did not date from the industrial era, nor the aftermath of either of the two World Wars, but from a rupture of the centuries-long cycle of intergenerational transmission of the Christian faith.

Most mainline Christian writers seem to have been swept along by this tidal wave of dissatisfaction, demanding change with a stridency that now seems to have been fuelled by rhetoric, rather than careful and responsible reflection. Slogans such as 'We must change or we shall die!' were the accepted wisdom of progressives within the Church of England and elsewhere. It is one thing to recognize the need for change, but what sort of change is required?

The publication of Robinson's *Honest to God* on 19 March 1963 mapped out a radical programme for change. Although clearly intended to be read by a wide public, its often opaque language caused many of its lay readers considerable difficulty. Technical theological terms were used without any explanation or contextualization. What on earth was the intended audience – who we must assume would be largely unchurched – to make of the assertion that 'popular supranaturalistic Christology has always been dominantly docetic'. The term 'docetic' is not explained. Theologians are introduced on the assumption that its audience will know exactly who they are. On the first page of the first chapter, we have a reference to 'Schleiermacher'. No attempt is made to explain who this writer is, or even provide his full name. I assume a graduate in theology could handle the text. But this does not seem to be the audience that Robinson has in mind.

The work attracted particular attention on account of the fact that its author was a bishop in the Church of England. Shortly before the publication of the book, Robinson had contributed an article to a leading English Sunday newspaper with the provocative title: 'Our Image of God must go'. When the book appeared, it became a bestseller in England,

and earned the nickname 'Honest John' for its author.[5] The initial print run ordered by the publishers was a mere 8,000 copies, of which 2,000 were intended for export to the United States. The print run was sold out on the first day of publication. The demand for the book took everyone by surprise. It is estimated that the book sold 350,000 copies during its first seven months.

SCM Press immodestly (and rather unwisely) went on to claim that it was 'the best-known religious book of the twentieth century';[6] a somewhat premature claim, resting on the assumption, which I am sure was entirely natural to its London publisher, that the entire world still talked about nothing but British books. Yet such inflationary statements aside, there is no doubt that *Honest to God* had a major impact on English Christianity, especially Anglicanism, during the 1960s.

Its impact on the public impression of traditional Christian beliefs was generally rather negative. They came to be seen as outdated, meaningless relics of a bygone era. The Archbishop of Canterbury denounced the book for caricaturing the ordinary Christian's view of God. 'It is utterly wrong and misleading', he stated in a television interview on Sunday 1 April 1963, to reject 'the imagery of God held by Christian men, women and children: imagery that they have got from Jesus himself, the image of God the Father in heaven, and to say that we can't have any new thought until it is swept away.'

Robinson himself was surprised, and even distressed, by the response of the Church to his approach. As his personal correspondence makes clear, he saw himself as an apologist – one whose calling is to restate the Christian faith in terms that make sense to those outside the Church. Having read *Honest to God* thoroughly and carefully, I can entirely understand his reaction. Robinson's vision is that of a reformulated Christianity, stated in terms that will resonate with 'modern man'. I would judge that such a 'modern man' would have some difficulty in making sense of the work at many points, due to Robinson's donnish habit of assuming that his audience is theologically literate – at least, in relation to authors he holds in esteem. But this is not my concern. In this essay, I want to explore Robinson's approach to the identity and significance of Jesus, and ask what its significance might be for the mission of the Church today.

Robinson's Apologetic Christology

The core of Robinson's views on how best to present Jesus to the modern world is found in the fourth chapter of *Honest to God*, entitled 'The Man for Others'. It is not the best chapter in the work, and it would be manifestly unfair to judge the book as a whole on the basis of this rather disappointing treatment of its critically important topic.

Its general tone is established by the end of its first page. Traditional Christology, we are told, 'has worked with a frankly supernaturalist scheme'.[7] Robinson's argument proceeds on the assumption that 'modern man' is not very enthusiastic about this sort of thing, and that we must therefore restate it in more acceptable forms. This, however, is a cultural, not a theological, judgement. What is worrying is that Robinson seems unable to appreciate the difference.

Most Christian apologists hold that the task of apologetics is to present a careful statement of the Christian faith using such cultural and intellectual vehicles that enable it to gain a hearing in contemporary culture, without reducing or distorting the gospel in order to do so. This includes the careful explanation of the status of religious language, including analogies and metaphors. Robinson's approach is to argue that many of the traditional doctrinal affirmations concerning Jesus must be set aside, in favour of modern, demythologized alternatives in the tradition of Bultmann or Tillich. Thus the traditional concepts of incarnation[8] and atonement[9] – to note but two particularly luminous doctrines – are declared to be in urgent need of reworking, to remove their unacceptable 'supernaturalist' elements.

Robinson assists his own argument through a presentation of the Chalcedonian Definition that seems designed to portray it as a piece of buffoonery. Without actually citing the Chalcedonian Definition – he provides a footnote reference to Bettenson's *Documents of the Christian Church* for those wishing to take it further – Robinson suggests that a convenient analogy will be sufficient to persuade us of the problems it raises.

> To use an analogy; if one had to present the doctrine of the person of Christ as a union of oil and water, then it made the best possible attempt to do so. Or rather, it made the only possible attempt, which was to insist that all efforts to 'confuse the substance' that there were two distinct natures and against all temptation to break the unity that there was but one indivisible person.[10]

By this stage, the lay reader may well be disinclined to take the orthodox notion with any great seriousness. Presumably this was Robinson's intention in using such a misleading analogy, which may indeed mirror the Chalcedonian concept of 'two natures', but completely fails to deal with the equally significant concept of 'one person and substance'. Robinson draws from this the conclusion that this is an inherently improbable and unstable model:

> It is not surprising, however, that in popular Christianity the oil and water separated, and that one or the other came to the top. In fact, popular supernaturalist Christology has always been dominantly docetic. That is to say, Christ only appeared to be a man or looked like a man: 'underneath' he was God.[11]

In evaluating this analogy, we shall have to set aside the minor scientific detail that, since oil is lighter than water, it will invariably rise to the surface, irrespective of the historical or cultural situation. Nor does Robinson make it clear whether we are to understand that the oil is the analogue of Christ's humanity, and the water of his divinity; or the inverse.

Yet the simple fact is that Robinson's analogy does not for one moment point to the emergence of the *docetic* heresy. The analogy does not deny that both water and oil are really present; the issue is which is the more visible – or, to put it another way, which is possessed of a more accentuated visibility. Robinson's argument might certainly lead to what might reasonably be styled a 'Nestorian' Christology, with its uneasy resolution of the relation of the two natures through the device of the 'union of good pleasure', or perhaps a variant of the Alexandrian position, such as Apollinarianism, through its emphasis upon the divinity of Christ (which was not understood to entail the denial of his humanity) – but certainly not its docetic cousin. This misrepresentation of the situation arises only partly from the weakness of the analogy Robinson presents; it is more fundamentally due to a misreading of the patristic debates over the identity of Christ.

That misreading continues in a highly rhetorical passage, in which Robinson insists that the Chalcedonian approach leads to the notion of Christ as 'a divine visitant from "out there", who chooses to live in every respect like the natives'.[12] I have no doubt that this is the consequence of a kenotic or docetic Christology;[13] yet it is most emphatically not the implication of the strongly incarnational Chalcedonian Christology. Robinson's criticism here rests upon his inferring of such corollaries of the Chalcedonian Definition that none of its traditional representatives would recognize. I am unable to discern whether this misconstrual arises from the polemical rhetoric of this section of the book, or a more fundamental misunderstanding of the traditional position. Certainly, Robinson notes that the position is widely misunderstood in society at large, and even within the Church. However, the trajectory of his argument implies that he does not himself labour under this disadvantage.

So what does Robinson offer in the place of this allegedly outdated way of understanding Jesus? At first sight, he offers a most attractive strategy: returning to the New Testament.[14] Robinson was an excellent New Testament scholar,[15] and this would seem to point to a highly promising way of proceeding. New Testament scholarship, then as now, offered some highly significant ways of reconceptualizing the identity of Jesus, not least by stripping away the exiguous metaphysics of an earlier generation, and identifying what it is about Jesus that requires to be formulated and proclaimed in today's context.[16]

Yet there is virtually no indication of this scholarly competence or expertise in this chapter – nor, I regret to say, at other points in the book at which it might reasonably have been expected to surface, with profit. Robinson's account of the New Testament material is deeply disappointing. It fails to even begin to deal with the issues of New Testament interpretation that led the Church to the Chalcedonian formula, offering a frankly rather simplistic dismissal of such claims on the basis of a puzzlingly selective and limited engagement with New Testament passages. The bottom line of Robinson's rather opaque argument seems to be that 'Jesus never claims to be God, personally; yet he always claims to bring God, completely.'[17] There is a worrying assumption here that one may speak of function without reflecting on identity – almost as if an a priori embargo has been placed on the process of metaphysical reflection and exploration.

Robinson here illustrates well the theological evasion of metaphysics, characteristic of this era, which is perhaps most evident in its Christological debates. There was no shortage of those during the 1960s urging the elimination of such metaphysical categories as static and outdated, insisting instead on an ontological atheism.[18] A functional approach to Christology is seen by some as legitimizing a focus on what Jesus Christ can be said to have done or achieved, without entailing any awkward metaphysical questions. By suggesting that Jesus 'brings God', Robinson believes, we can avoid being theologically *serious*, asking the fundamental question: who must Jesus *be* if Jesus is able to *do* this? If Jesus is the bearer of God, who is Jesus? It requires only a modest knowledge of historical theology to be aware that the early church debated this issue at length, before reaching their resolution of the issues involved. Their reflections must give us pause for thought, in that they indicate that ontology and function are far more completely and inalienably intertwined than Robinson's brief and rather dismissive analysis suggests.

As Richard Bauckham has shown, on the basis of a detailed examination of critical passages, the simple model that separates out 'function' and 'ontology' is quite unrealistic.

> The dominance of the distinction between 'functional' and 'ontic' Christology has made it seem unproblematic to say that for early Christology Jesus exercises the 'functions' of Lordship without being regarded as 'ontologically' divine. In fact, such a distinction is highly problematic from the point of view of early Jewish monotheism, for in this understanding of the unique divine identity, the unique sovereignty of God was not a mere 'function' which God could delegate to someone else. It was one of the key identifying characteristics of the unique divine identity, which distinguishes the one God from all other reality.[19]

For Bauckham, the New Testament 'identifies Jesus as intrinsic to who God is'.[20] The New Testament may not make significant use of the language of metaphysics; it nevertheless prepared the ground for those who realized that such categories would be needed to contain the new wine of the gospel proclamation. This naturally leads to the view that the New Testament contains the fundamental themes and pointers, in embryonic form, which would eventually lead to the Nicene theology of the fourth century. This theology thus brings to full and conscious articulation the somewhat more tentative metaphysical hints of the New Testament, developing – not distorting – them in doing so.[21]

As a historical theologian, I was deeply concerned by Robinson's misreading of Chalcedon, evident throughout *Honest to God*, and especially in its fourth chapter. Robinson appears to believe that orthodox Christianity has shut down discussion of the identity of Jesus and the best means of proclaiming this in different cultural contexts, locking it in to an outmoded 'supernaturalist' mode of thought. Yet even the most traditionalist of Christian writers insist that Chalcedon marks the beginning, not the end, of such an engagement. As Karl Rahner has argued, Chalcedon thus represents a beginning rather than an end, in that it lays down a 'line of demarcation' on essentials, while leaving open the question how lesser issues are to be addressed and understood.[22] For Rahner, none of the Church's dogmatic formulas can claim to be the last word on matters; nevertheless, Chalcedon established a basic framework within which the *mysterium Christi* could be explored further, while remaining within what the community of faith regarded as its authentic limits. Rahner himself deplored the formulaic approaches to Christology that Chalcedon seemed to inspire, and urged a recovery of its deeper meaning (especially in relation to the humanity of Christ) through a process of dynamic engagement with the tradition, and a reappropriation of its central living themes.

A similar point is made by E. L. Mascall, who argues that while 'the Definition of Chalcedon is the truth and nothing but the truth', it is also necessary to insist that 'it is not the whole truth'.[23] Its basic insights determine a starting point and means of proceeding, rather than conclude a discussion of its full significance.

> [Chalcedon] both needs and is patent of much more exploration and extension than it has in fact received. It may well be that the very authority which it has been accorded in Christendom has led to it being treated too often as a static and finished product and to its potentialities for development being ignored.[24]

It can be argued that the decision to adopt the specific metaphysical categories associated with the Chalcedonian Definition was linked with the specific social and historical location of the Church at the time.[25] This would leave the Church in subsequent eras free to choose which metaphysical categories were best adapted to the contingencies of their periods, rather than limiting them to those definitively set out at Nicaea. Karl Rahner, for example, argued for the recognition of corrective replacements of historically conditioned theological formulations, and in his later writings, pressed for the translation of traditional formulae into contemporary thought forms and modes of expression.[26] Yet I see no awareness of this issue in Robinson's account of traditional Christology, which he persists in portraying in the form of wooden stereotypes, such as the outdated 'supernaturalism' it allegedly embodies.[27]

The Problem of Cultural Change

In 1972, Stephen J. Gould and Niles Eldredge proposed a theory of biological evolution which has since come to be known as 'punctuated equilibrium'.[28] This holds that most evolution occurs in short bursts, interspersed with long periods of stability. Gould and Eldredge attacked the idea that organisms continually change, adapting by small degrees to fit their environment. Where Charles Darwin had viewed evolution as a slow, continuous process, without sudden jumps, Gould and Eldredge noted that the fossils of organisms found in subsequent geological layers indicated long intervals in which nothing changed (hence 'equilibrium'), yet 'punctuated' by short, revolutionary transitions, in which species became extinct and are replaced by wholly new forms. New species appear in large numbers over short periods, perhaps because of dramatic events such as asteroid impacts. Gould – perhaps the most influential and best known evolutionary biologist since Charles Darwin – was widely criticized by more conventional Darwinists, who styled his theory 'evolution by jerks'.

A culture also undergoes change – sometimes slowly over many years, sometimes with such speed that the settled assumptions of generations are overthrown, even inverted, within a single generation. After periods of relative stability, massive change can take place, often without much warning that this is about to happen. What was entirely plausible in one cultural context now becomes seen as eccentric, possibly even irrational. The same belief may appear as the accepted wisdom of the age at one point, and 40 years later be regarded as hopelessly old-fashioned and outdated.

This is what has happened during the generation separating the publication of *Honest to God* in 1963 and 2003. The settled modernist assumptions of the 1960s – which Robinson faithfully echoes – have been overthrown by what often seems to be their systematic inversion. Modernity has died, and given way to postmodernity. And at point after point, we find that what modernity valued, postmodernity dismisses; what modernity critiqued, postmodernity affirms. The implications for the current-day relevance of Robinson's approach will be obvious. Robinson describes his approach as 'radical'; it is better described simply as 'modernist'. Robinson suggested that he would probably be judged not to have been radical enough.[29] I disagree. Robinson bought into modernism more than enough; a truly radical writer would have sought to disentangle Anglican Christianity from the modernist trap into which it had fallen, and allow it to rediscover some insights that it had lost. We should not have had to wait for postmodernity to rediscover the importance of the transcendent.

It is now clear that many of the more radical religious writings of the 1960s proposed agendas based on the interesting assumption that the prevailing modernist trends actually represented permanent changes in Western culture. It was a hasty and incorrect judgement. As Adrian Hastings points out, this period merely witnessed a temporary change of cultural mood, which some were unwise enough to treat as a fixed and lasting change in the condition of humanity:

> In retrospect the dominant theological mood of that time in its hasty, slack, rather collective sweep reminds one a little painfully of a flight of lemmings . . . A good deal of the more publicized theological writing in the sixties gives the impression of a sheer surge of feeling that in the modern world God, religion, the transcendent, any reliability in the gospels, anything which had formed part of the old 'supernatualist' system, had suddenly become absurd.[30]

As many of the dominant cultural trends of this era were still shaped by the Enlightenment, this had the regrettable consequence that the radical new visions of Christianity being proposed were often shaped by rationalist assumptions, which the rise of post-modernity would largely sweep away.

The influence of the Enlightenment on the theological experimentations of the 1960s was significant, possibly even decisive. It lingered on in more reactionary theological circles, even into the late 1970s. The contributors to *The Myth of God Incarnate* (1977) seem to have regarded the Enlightenment as something that was given and fixed for all time. Leslie Houlden, one of the more influential of its contributors, argued that we have no option but to accept the rationalist outlook of the Enlightenment, and restructure our Christian thinking accordingly. 'We must accept our lot, bequeathed to us by the Enlightenment, and make the most of it.'[31] Yet even as Houlden was writing, the Enlightenment world-view was dying. The paradox of *The Myth of God Incarnate* was that it mingled a desire for theological innovation with a somewhat uncritical perpetuation of the fundamental (and thoroughly backward-looking) themes of modernity that severely limited the options for such innovation. What happened was that 'modern churchmen' chose to set off down a road that postmodern people would regard as implausible, outdated and unattractive.

The importance of this point cannot be overlooked. While loose talk of 'radical cultural change' is generally unhelpful, there can be little doubt that some highly significant changes have taken place in British culture between the years 1963 and 2003. The most significant is the death of the Enlightenment, and the rise of postmodernity, both as a somewhat unreflective cultural mood and as a more sophisticated intellectual project. A generation of Christians who had invested their professional careers in making Christianity relevant and meaningful by the standards and norms of the Enlightenment found that their lifelong labours had been something of a waste of time. Postmodernity rather liked the kind of mystical spiritualities that the Enlightenment derided and deplored as illogical and irrational.

A generation of post-war English theologians thus created an unusable past for the Christian tradition. What modernity applauded, postmodernity excoriated. The demand for 'modern' beliefs merely led to an unwise theological investment in the Enlightenment, at a time when its currency was already becoming devalued in more perceptive circles. The level of exposure was so great that the theological fortunes of 'modern' belief were inextricably linked with that of the

Enlightenment in general. The quest for a 'secular faith' sounded just fine in the 1960s. Its emphasis on rationality resonated with the cultural mood of that atypical moment, as did its excoriation of such 'irrationalities' or 'superstitions' as the notion of 'mystery' or 'the transcendent'.

With the rise of postmodernity, however, a new interest blossomed in these spiritual categories, whereas 'rationalism' was derided as truncated, cold, insensitive and inattentive to the deeper levels of human existence and perception. Some theologians of the 1960s seem to have ended up creating a form of Christianity that would be lukewarmly welcomed in 1960, yet regarded as totally implausible in 2000. William Ralph Inge (1860–1954), one of England's wittier religious writers, once quipped that whoever married the spirit of the age today would be widowed tomorrow. The worrying contemporary *unusability* of so much English-language theology of the 1960s is a telling affirmation of the truth in that aphorism.

The agenda that John Robinson set himself in *Honest to God* is admirable. The effective communication of the faith is essential to the future of the Church. Robinson's apologetic strategy is clearly to restate the gospel in terms that make sense to the modern world. Robinson and I, of course, would use the word 'modern' in rather different senses. Robinson's entire project is grounded on the assumption that 'modern' means up to date; I take it to mean a transient world-view that held that it was self-evidently true, yet has suffered the embarrassment of being shown to be specific to a past period in history and culture. What Robinson offers his readers is a modernist reworking of traditional Christian beliefs. As E. L. Mascall pointed out, the result was somewhat predictable.

Restatement of the faith once delivered to the saints, however fresh, intelligent, and contemporary the language in which it might be expressed, has already been rejected as insufficiently radical to meet the situation. One might be pardoned for supposing that Robinson had despaired of trying to convert the world to Christianity and had decided instead to try to convert Christianity to the world. And this is what, as far as I can see, he would be committing himself to doing if he saw the full implication of his words.[32]

John Robinson's *Honest to God* is an illuminating period piece, enabling historians to catch something of the mood of the time, and the reactions that it evoked. It stands as a curious memorial to an equally puzzling period in the history of British Christianity, characterized by an impatience with the existing state of things, and a remorseless determination to change things. Yet the specifics of Robinson's approach are heavily conditioned by assumptions deriving from the Enlightenment. Have they a future? Many doubt it.

Many, that is, but not all. There is at least one figure who continues to see Robinson's agenda as significant – John Shelby Spong, who recently retired as the Episcopalian bishop of Newark, New Jersey. In an important article in the September 1993 edition of *The Voice*, the newspaper of the Diocese of Newark, Spong explained at some length how he had been inspired by Robinson's work since first reading *Honest to God* in 1965. At that stage, he was rector of Calvary Chapel in Tarboro, the county seat of Edgecombe County, North Carolina.

I did not rush to read the book. Reviews indicated that it quoted extensively from Rudolf Bultmann, Dietrich Bonhoeffer, and Paul Tillich. I was quite familiar with these thinkers and so I dismissed the book as a popularizing effort of no great significance. Nonetheless I placed the book on my reading schedule, and finally got to it in 1965. I remember the day I first opened this book. Vacationing on the Outer Banks of North Carolina, I sat on the beach one afternoon with *Honest to God*. I did not put it down until I had read it through three times. I knew from that moment that my life would never be the same.

Spong clearly saw himself as the American equivalent of Bishop Robinson, and welcomed reviews that encouraged the comparison. He was particularly appreciative of the invitation he received from *Christian Century* to write the tribute to Robinson after his death in 1983. In Spong's view, *Honest to God* demanded the rejection of 'childish' versions of the Christian faith.

John Robinson made me aware that my childhood under-standing of God would not live in my world. He forced me to face the fact that the words of both the Bible and the Creeds sound strange to post-modern people and that my faith had to grow or it had to be abandoned. I began on that day the long, tortuous and, to this moment, not yet completed process of rethinking all of the symbols of my religious past so that I could continue to claim them with integrity.

The influence of Robinson's work on Spong is best seen in his 1998 work *Why Christianity must Change or Die: A Bishop Speaks to Believers in Exile*. In this work, Spong sets out 12 theses for a new 'Reformation', as follows:

1. Theism as a way of defining God, is dead. God can no longer be understood with credibility as a Being, supernatural in power, dwelling above the sky and prepared to invade human history periodically to enforce the divine will. So, most theological talk today is meaningless unless we find a new way to speak of God.

2. Since God can no longer be conceived in theistic terms, it becomes nonsensical to seek to understand Jesus as the

incarnation of the theistic deity. So the Christology of the ages is bankrupt.

3. The biblical story of the perfect and finished creation from which human beings fell into sin is pre-Darwinian mythology and post-Darwinian nonsense.

4. The virgin birth, understood as literal biology, makes the divinity of Christ, as traditionally understood, impossible.

5. The miracle stories of the New Testament can no longer be interpreted in a post-Newtonian world as supernatural events performed by an incarnate deity.

6. The view of the cross as a sacrifice for the sins of the world is a barbarian idea based on primitive concepts of God that must be dismissed.

7. Resurrection is an action of God, who raised Jesus into the meaning of God. It therefore cannot be a physical resuscitation occurring inside human history.

8. The story of the ascension assumed a three-tiered universe and is therefore not capable of being translated into the concepts of a post-Copernican space age.

9. There is no external, objective, revealed standard writ in Scripture or on tablets of stone that will govern our ethical behaviour for all time.

10. Prayer cannot be a request made to a theistic deity to act in human history in a particular way.

11. The hope for life after death must be separated for ever from the behavior-control mentality of reward and punishment. The church must abandon, therefore, its reliance on guilt as a motivator of behavior.

12. All human beings bear God's image and must be respected for what each person is. Therefore no external description of one's being, whether based on race, ethnicity, gender or sexual orientation, can properly be used as the basis for either rejection or discrimination.[33]

What is interesting is that nine of these twelve theses can

unambiguously be traced back to Robinson's seminal work, as follows: 1. The denial of theism;[34] 2. the rejection of the divinity of Jesus;[35] 3. the denial of the creation story along with the Fall;[36] 4. the rejection of the virgin birth;[37] 5. the rejection of the miracles attributed to Jesus;[38] 6. the rejection of traditional understandings of the atonement made by Christ on the cross;[39] 8. the rejection of the ascension of Christ as resting on an outmoded cosmology;[40] 9. the rejection of fixed ethical systems;[41] 10. the denial of the efficacy of prayer directed towards God.[42] It will, of course, be clear that five of these are explicitly Christological. Interestingly, Spong's critique of the resurrection does not follow Robinson, but seems to rest on an aspect of Bultmann's theology thay Robinson chose not to develop.

It is therefore entirely fair to suggest that the apologetic strategy set out in Robinson's *Honest to God* has reached its high noon in the writings of John Shelby Spong. There are significant differences between their approaches: where Robinson is at points tentative and exploratory, for example, Spong is rather more strident and categorical. The predominant trend within British Anglican apologetics has been to tread the road set out so carefully by writers such as Dorothy L. Sayers and C. S. Lewis.[43] E. L. Mascall once noted 'the extreme trouble' that Sayers took 'to ensure that what she was trying to express in contemporary idiom was the authentic teaching of Christianity'.[44] Robinson's approach is quite distinct: that of 'restating' the Christian tradition – something which involved such radical revision that, for many, the outcome was simply not recognizable as Christian orthodoxy. But this approach lives on; Bishop Spong is the new Bishop Robinson.

Conclusion

In this essay, I have taken a critical view of Robinson's *Honest to God*, noting the rapid cultural erosion of its approach, which renders it of little use to the Church of today, and expressing concerns about the plausibility of both the criticisms he directs against traditional Christology, and the somewhat puzzling alternatives that he proposes. The work is to be valued as an exhibit in a museum of historical theology, a fascinating witness to the cultural mood of a bygone era, and a failed strategy to respond to it. Robinson challenges us to respond to our new situation. Even though I believe that his strategy was flawed at the time, and has been rendered unusable through the erosion of the principles that he regarded as self-evident, I have no doubt that we must heed his challenge to speak to the '"lay" world' in terms it can understand[45] – but also in terms that remain faithful to the Christian tradition.

NOTES

1 This approach can be seen throughout the three volumes of my *Scientific Theology*, published by T. & T. Clark. The three volumes are *Nature* (2001), *Reality* (2002) and *Theory* (2003).

2 Tom Wolfe, 'The Great Relearning', in *Hooking Up*, Jonathan Cape, 2000, pp. 140–5.

3 For reflections, see Arthur Marwick, *The Sixties: Cultural Revolution in Britain, France, Italy, and the United States, c.1958–c.1974*, Oxford University Press, 1998.

4 Callum Brown, *The Death of Christian Britain*, Routledge, 2000.

5 For background, see Eric James, *A Life of Bishop John A. T. Robinson*, Collins, 1987. For an analysis of the reaction, see David L. Edwards, *The Honest to God Debate*, SCM Press, 1963.

6 I am using the 1974 printing of the work, which includes this inflationary claim on the back cover. References throughout this chapter are to John A. T. Robinson, *Honest to God*, SCM Press, 1974.

7 Robinson, *Honest to God*, p. 64.

8 Robinson, *Honest to God*, pp. 65–70.

9 Robinson, *Honest to God*, pp. 77–9.
10 Robinson, *Honest to God*, p. 65.
11 Robinson, *Honest to God*, p. 65.
12 Robinson, *Honest to God*, p. 67.
13 Robinson himself appears sympathetic to the intentions of a kenotic approach, while noting its failings: *Honest to God*, pp. 74–5.
14 Robinson, *Honest to God*, pp. 70–5.
15 See, for example, his earlier work John A. T. Robinson, *Twelve New Testament Studies*, SCM Press, 1965. Later works include J. A. T. Robinson, *Redating the New Testament*, SCM Press, 1993.
16 There is an embarrassment of riches here: I think of works such as C. F. D. Moule, *The Origin of Christology*, Cambridge University Press, 1997.
17 Robinson, *Honest to God*, p. 73.
18 This is the position of the Canadian philosopher Leslie Dewart, also writing in the 1960s. See his *The Future of Belief: Theism in a World Come of Age*, Burns & Oates, 1967; idem, *The Foundations of Belief*, Burns & Oates, 1969. For an assessment of his views, see Desmond Connell, 'Professor Dewart and Dogmatic Development', *Irish Theological Quarterly* 34, 1967, pp. 309–28; 35, 1968, pp. 33–57 and 117–40.
19 Richard Bauckham, *God Crucified: Monotheism and Christology in the New Testament*, Eerdmans, 1998, p. 41.
20 Bauckham, *God Crucified*, p. 42.
21 The basic issues and some of the concerns they raise are set out fully in Winfried Schulz, *Dogmenentwicklung als Problem der Geschichtlichkeit der Wahrheitserkenntnis. Eine erkenntnistheoretisch-theologische Studie zum Problemkreis der Dogmenentwicklung*, Libreria Editrice dell'Università Gregoriana, 1969.
22 Karl Rahner, 'Chalkedon – Ende oder Anfang?', in Alois Grillmeier and Heinrich Bacht (eds), *Das Konzil von Chalkedon: Geschichte und Gegenwart*, three vols., Echter-Verlag, 1951–54, vol. 3, pp. 3–49.
23 E. L. Mascall, 'On from Chalcedon', in *Whatever happened to the Human Mind? Essays in Orthodoxy*, SPCK, 1980, pp. 28–53, especially 28–9.
24 Mascall, 'On from Chalcedon', p. 37.
25 Avery Dulles, *The Survival of Dogma: Faith, Authority and Dogma in a Changing World*, Crossroad, 1982.
26 Karl Rahner, 'Zur Frage der Dogmenentwicklung', in *Schriften zur Theologie*, Benziger Verlag, 1954, vol. 1, pp. 49–90; idem, 'Überlegungen zur Dogmenentwicklung', in *Schriften zur Theologie*, Benziger Verlag, 1960, vol. 4, pp. 11–50.

27 For an extended criticism of this misleading and inadequate notion in Robinson's analysis, see E. L. Mascall, *The Secularization of Christianity*, Darton, Longman and Todd, 1965, pp. 190–212.

28 S. J. Gould and N. Eldredge, 'Punctuated Equilibria: The Tempo and Mode of Evolution Reconsidered', *Paleobiology* 3, 1977, pp. 115–51. For a fuller statement of the theory, see Niles Eldredge, *The Pattern of Evolution*, Freeman, 1999; Stephen Jay Gould, *The Structure of Evolutionary Theory*, Belknap, 2002.

29 *Honest to God*, p. 10.

30 Adrian Hastings, *A History of English Christianity 1920–1985*, Collins, 1986, p. 545.

31 Leslie Houlden, in John Hick (ed.), *The Myth of God Incarnate*, SCM Press, 1977, p. 125.

32 Mascall, *The Secularization of Christianity*, p. 109.

33 Paraphrased from John Shelby Spong, *Why Christianity must Change or Die: A Bishop Speaks to Believers in Exile*, HarperSanFrancisco, 1998, *passim*.

34 *Honest to God*, pp. 40–1.

35 *Honest to God*, pp. 67–75.

36 *Honest to God*, pp. 33–4.

37 *Honest to God*, pp. 65–8.

38 *Honest to God*, pp. 35 and 68.

39 *Honest to God*, p. 78.

40 *Honest to God*, p. 11.

41 *Honest to God*, pp. 105–21. Robinson here draws rather uncritically on the 'situation ethics' of Joseph Fletcher. For their full statement, see Joseph Fletcher, *Situation Ethics: The New Morality*, SCM Press, 1966. Robinson bases himself on a 1959 article laying down the broad outlines of this approach.

42 See the discussion in *Honest to God*, pp. 84–105

43 Both of whom Robinson notes in *Honest to God*, p. 15.

44 Mascall, *The Secularization of Christianity*, p. 107.

45 *Honest to God*, p. 8.

8. 'To Bring God Completely':

Honest to God and Christology for the Twenty-first Century

JANE WILLIAMS

Mission and Mediation

Honest to God was intended to make Christianity stronger in Britain. In his preface to the book, John Robinson makes it clear that, in his experience at least, many people were rejecting not Christianity itself but 'a particular way of thinking about the world which quite legitimately they find incredible'.[1] It is not Christianity itself, he argues, that is incredible, but just the way in which it is expressed.

It is important to bear this in mind from the start of this exploration of Christology in the light of *Honest to God*: Robinson is not questioning the truth of the faith in which he grew up and to which he dedicated his life. He saw himself as standing in the apostolic line of those who were called to teach and defend the faith by making it comprehensible for his contemporaries. This process is an inevitable part of Christian witness. The writers of the New Testament were doing it when they tried to tell the story of Jesus in ways that would be understood by those who were not brought up as Jews. The fathers of the Church were doing it when they declared that Christ is 'of one being with the Father'.[2] Every preacher who stands up in the pulpit and illustrates her sermon with a

contemporary metaphor is doing it. Christians are irrevoca-
bly involved in walking the tightrope between faithfulness to
what has been received and the unavoidable call to preach the
gospel to our own culture.

Robinson is sure that his approach is not the only one
possible for church leaders.[3] But he is also sure that it is what
he himself is called to. He acknowledges, with moving honesty,
that he is talking not only to intelligent sceptics outside the
Church, but also to himself.[4] A significant proportion of the
massive correspondence that ensued after the publication of
Honest to God suggested that John was talking for many other
Christians, as well. Many of the more critical responses the
book received seemed particularly scandalized that a *bishop*
should write such a book, whereas John thought that it was
precisely because he was a bishop that he was required to take
up the challenge of trying to discern how best to guard and
defend the faith.[5]

But there is no point in simply 'guarding' Christianity. It is a
gospel, a proclamation of good news, not a historic heirloom,
and it demands to be preached, not kept in a case. This task of
finding the right words to make the good news come alive is
the first task that *Honest to God* set itself.

But the second was to be faithful to what has traditionally
been claimed about the relationship between Jesus and God.
John always claimed to be a radical, rather than a liberal, and
certainly the Christology of *Honest to God* is attempting to
get back to the roots of these claims about Jesus. It is not
assuming that the whole idea of God or of incarnation are
incredible to the modern mind, but only that the way in which
those truths are expressed must change.

So *Honest to God* is also attempting a mediating task. This
is particularly clear in the Christological Chapter 4, 'The Man
for Others'. Robinson is rejecting both unthinking reitera-
tion of old formulae and mindless rejection of all that the
formulae encapsulate. He rejects a Christology that suggests

that someone from 'out there' has somehow to be got 'into' a human body. But he also rejects any solution that leaves the divine out of the equation altogether.[6] So Chapter 4 of *Honest to God* is looking for a way of saying how Jesus makes God uniquely present in the human situation, without using the language of the creed, so without talking about 'of one substance' or 'fully God and fully man'. He is attempting to mediate between orthodoxy and a simplistic rejection of orthodoxy, in order to find a gospel that can be preached and heard.

'The Man for Others'

The problem that John identifies in the Christology of the Creed is what he calls 'supranaturalism' – someone coming 'from out there'. In most Christian preaching, he suggests, this turns into a kind of mythology, not significantly different from, for example, the ancient classical myths of gods who come down and mingle with mortals for a while. This Christology is essentially 'docetic', meaning that the humanity of Jesus is basically just a disguise or a cover story. The divine is the real actor, and is unaffected by its temporary wearing of a human form. As a matter of fact, as John acknowledges, the traditional formula worked out at the Council of Chalcedon in 451 rules out that kind of mythology in favour of a rigorous metaphysic of a union of real humanity and real divinity that preserves the full reality of both. But this philosophical statement loses a great deal in most pulpits.

If the way in which Jesus brings the presence of God into the human situation is one area where 'supranaturalism' has disabled the preaching of the gospel to the modern era, in John's opinion, the other is the atonement. God's saving action on the cross, John argues, is generally described in ways that are 'frankly incredible'. God's intervention is, he says, described in terms of the way in which we would put our 'finger into a glass of water to rescue a struggling insect'.[7]

So *Honest to God* is looking for a solution to the problem of 'supranaturalism' that does not entail rejecting all the truths that these 'mythical' descriptions enshrine. Robinson does not reject the uniqueness of Christ, or the completeness of God's activity through him. His examination of the Gospels – a surprisingly brief study, for a New Testament scholar – leads him to the conclusion that 'Jesus never claims to be God, personally: yet he always claims to bring God, completely.'[8] So this must be the starting point for our Christology, too. Is this claim of Jesus' justified, and if so, how?

Robinson takes his answers very largely from Bonhoeffer and Tillich, or his interpretation of them. The way forward, Robinson argues, is one that sees incarnation and atonement as essentially the same process, whereby human beings become increasingly 'at one' with the ground of their being. In Jesus we see a man who is so wholly given to God that there is no separation.

Robinson quotes quite large chunks, particularly of Tillich, which describe the human state of alienation from each other and from the 'origin and aim of our life', and the experience of 'grace' breaking through to allow us to know that '*You are accepted*'.[9]

This largely experiential and emotional description of the atonement is then cobbled together, not wholly successfully, with a few of Bonhoeffer's more radical statements about the suffering of God, and the Christian calling to share in that powerlessness and suffering. Robinson glosses over the fact that the two accounts he has described are largely antithetical, and that, at least in the portion of Tillich that he has used, there is no obvious necessity for the cross at all, whereas in Bonhoeffer it is central to the whole understanding of the way of God in the world. Robinson believes that he has offered a 'natural' account of the humanity of Jesus, fully given to God and so fully transparent to the love of God. He also believes that he has offered a Christology that leads to a call to a particular kind of Christian ethical discipleship. Where people live together in unselfish relatedness, there is the new creation, Robinson argues.

Solving the Right Problem?

If this is the solution that Robinson offers to the problem he has identified, the first question must be, did he correctly identify the problem? His correspondents, who were legion, were divided, and it is quite hard for modern commentators to feel themselves back into the mood of the early 1960s. As Rowan Williams says in his essay on '*Honest to God* in Great Britain', '*Honest to God* could only have been written by an Anglican at such a moment in history.'[10] Despite its use of Bonhoeffer and Tillich, it is indeed a curiously British book.

One of the symptoms of that is some uncertainty about who is being addressed by the book. Is it the Church of England church-goer? Is it the wider community, rather well read and with some interest in and knowledge of Christianity, or is it church leaders and academics? The way in which it was headlined in the papers and received by the public suggests that it was seen as a book that anybody in the nation might have an opinion about. In that sense, it is a book produced by someone deeply embedded in the mentality of a church for the nation, as Robinson was. He did not have to ask himself the question about potential readership, because the Church of England in the 1960s was still sufficiently a national church to excite interest even among those who never went to it.

In an article on 'British Theologies', Stephen Sykes has pointed out that since the nineteenth century British theology has largely been done in a secular university environment, without the assumptions about denominational norms or vocational training that have played a major role in the formation of continental theologians. Although this has, as Sykes acknowledges, strengths, the major weakness that he identifies is in the area of systematics and dogmatics.[11] Robinson's discussion of God-language seems to assume that no such questions have been asked before, whereas there is of course a huge and sophisticated Christian tradition of asking just such questions.[12] But the point is not to criticize Robinson for failing to refer to this tradition but to note that his assumption about his audience's ignorance of it was surely correct.

Another reflection of the way in which *Honest to God* arises out of the state of British theology is the very small role played by the Christian community in the book. This is perhaps particularly odd for a man who had made a considerable name for himself as a liturgist while Dean of Clare College, Cambridge. Worship, sacrament, prayer, spirituality, discipleship – all the hallmarks of the context in which, as a matter of fact, doctrine has always been done by Christians – all receive at best an honourable mention. They do not affect the substance of the argument.[13] If one compares this with, for example, Bonhoeffer, it is becomes clear why this is such a serious omission. In Bonhoeffer, discipleship and community are the essential response to the work of God in Christ and the place where that work continues to be an effective challenge to 'religion'. Robinson's book is clearly talking about problems with 'religion', which is a system for reducing the divine action to something usable and comfortable for human beings. The God of Bonhoeffer's 'religionless Christianity' is always outside any such systems, and the only response to him is obedience such as Christ's.

Again, Robinson is not to be chastised for failing to do a systematic reading of Bonhoeffer. All that Robinson had in front of him at the time was *Letters and Papers from Prison*, a tantalizing and inevitably sporadic set of writings. Bonhoeffer had tragically little time to write a systematic theology at all, but his biographer, Eberhard Bethge, acknowledges that it was partly Robinson's book that spurred Bonhoeffer's friends into collecting and publishing talks and lectures, thereby giving us broader insights into how the themes from *Letters and Papers from Prison* might have fitted into a fuller theology.[14] But whereas it was obvious to Bonhoeffer that the witnessing community is the locus of true theology, to Robinson, writing in Britain in the 1960s, that was apparently not so obvious. Bonhoeffer sees the 'problem' for his time and his nation as a problem of 'religiousness' that does not obviously bear witness to Jesus Christ today.[15] For him, then, the only possible solution is a lived one.

In contrast, Robinson's sketch of the problem and answer are curiously cerebral. It may tell us quite a bit about Robinson himself that he saw the problem as essentially one of language. If we get the language about God right, people will see and believe. But if this appealed to Robinson, writer and academic, a shy man who communicated most vitally through the written word, it is also the solution offered by large numbers of others. The Church of England has gone through any number of liturgical revisions presumably in the belief that language can be converting or off-putting. Campaigners for women's liberation or for the recognition of equal rights for black people or the disabled all target language as part of the necessary process of change. Language does shape belief and imagination in fundamental ways. But language and praxis also interact, so that it is very doubtful which is chicken and which is egg, which changes which. Perhaps the two always have to go together?

It would be quite unfair to suggest that Robinson was only interested in Christian language. There is, for example, the section on morality in *Honest to God* that clearly assumes that faith and life have to go together. But the Christological section, which is my primary concern in this essay, is striking for its lack of emphasis on the Jesus movement.

Our Problem, Our Solution?

But, while it is fascinating to read *Honest to God* in its historical context, and try to work out how effectively it did the
missionary job it set out to do at that time, the real point of
this symposium is actually to look at the issues raised for us
now. If Robinson identified a declining interest in Christianity
in the 1960s, how much more must we now admit that, at
least in Britain, Christianity is a minority religion that fails
to attract new converts even at a rate to keep up with those
leaving the Church. Is this because we still have not addressed
the problems of 'supranaturalism', as described by Robinson,
or are his detractors right in saying that he and his ilk have
hastened the decline of Christianity by evacuating the
language of all content? Or perhaps both of these alternatives
are oversimplistic?

Inevitably, in trying to assess the problem and suggest a
solution for today, my essay will be as personal as Robinson's
was. If he admitted that he was preaching to people like himself,
I must do the same. My suggestions may look as off-beam to
some as Robinson's did, and the temptation is not even to
try, knowing that the chances of my lighting on a universal
solution are nil. But in what follows, defeatism is one of the
things for which I will castigate my contemporaries, so I had
probably better not give into it immediately myself.

Let me begin by stating boldly that I do not believe that
'supranaturalism' is any longer – if it ever was – the main barrier
to belief. I do not believe that people find the basic tenets of
Christianity incredible, in theory, but only in practice.[16] Ours
is a far less severely rational time than the 1960s, and I would
argue that that could be demonstrated in almost any sphere
of human knowledge. Science, theology, imagination, the arts
are all far more interdependent than they would have been
40 years ago. Whether you look at what we read, what we
watch, what peoples our worlds of the imagination, or how
we use language, I think it is clear that people today, by and

large, are far more comfortable with the inexplicable and mysterious than Robinson's contemporaries. They are also, arguably, more at home with religious-sounding questions in everyday life. And although many Christians would be very uncertain about how useful it is to us that our contemporaries might believe in visitors from other planets, or healings that are not explicable in strictly medical terms, nonetheless, the fact remains that 'supranaturalism' is not a no-go area. If we were happy to have Christianity considered as one of a number of slightly wacky but not impossible alternative lifestyles, we would find an easy home in Glastonbury or Bloomsbury.

So for Robinson's 'supranaturalism', I would substitute 'exclusivism' as the first of the major problems facing us today. It is not divine presence and activity that is impossible to believe, but the Christian claim that our telling of it is the only possible one.

Just as for Robinson, the doubts about 'supranaturalism' have knock-on effects on all major Christian doctrines, and particularly the atonement, so too does this problem of 'exclusivism'. There is continuing and widespread interest in and respect for Jesus, as a man with a unique vision of God, and one that enables others to draw closer to the God whom he calls 'father'. But when claims are made that it is *only* through Jesus that we can come to God, many in our society would reject this as patently untrue. The presence of other faith communities in our society has made this claim sound much harsher and ruder than it did in a society where few people knew anyone whose religious tradition was apparently being disenfranchised by Christian exclusivism. The cross of Christ, instead of being the unique ransom paid to take away the sins of the world, is usually interpreted as a political act, or a gesture of solidarity with the suffering and the outcast.

Strong theologies of the cross, such as liberation theology, or the theology of Jürgen Moltmann, do seem to allow avenues of approach to the atonement that make sense of it to contemporaries, in a way that was not available to Robinson. Moltmann's *The Crucified God*, for example, suggests that the cross is best read as identifying the power of God with those abandoned by civil and religious authorities, and even by God himself.

'Jesus' way to the cross ended with open questions: with the question of the righteousness of God, between Jesus and the understanding of law in his time; with the question of the authority of freedom, between Jesus and the religio-political power of Rome; and with the question of the divinity of God, between Jesus and his Father.'[17] Moltmann suggests that these questions are answered by the resurrection, but that they are atonement questions, showing God's presence with the politically and religiously unacceptable, and with those who seem to be forsaken by God himself.

But while that perhaps provides a theory of the atonement that makes cultural sense to us, as classical theories did in their own time, it does nothing to deal directly with the charge of exclusivism. Nor does it, generally, face that charge head on. Is God's activity in the cross of Christ the only way in which God's presence is brought, redemptively, into situations of absence and forsakenness, or only a dramatic demonstration of what is already the case, and a demonstration that could be and is made by other means in other religious traditions? That is not a question that, as far as I know, is directly answered either by Moltmann or by liberation theologians.

This problem of 'exclusivism' is one that has been generated by what is usually called a 'postmodern' culture. Definitions of postmodernism are myriad, [18] but one of the characteristics agreed by all commentators is the rejection of a 'metanarrative'. We do not, culturally, believe that there is only one possible version of truth nowadays. We may not even believe that there is any such thing as 'truth' in an absolute sense, only a range of 'truths'. This suspicion of a master-story of the world has good and powerful roots in the history of the way in which dominant myths have been able to reject or rewrite the stories of the oppressed, and Christianity has not been historically innocent in this respect. But it is fundamental to Christianity to claim to be *the* metanarrative, the true story of the world. All too often, however, this has been coupled with an aggressive self-righteousness on the part of Christians themselves.

So perhaps an initial step towards engaging with the problem presented to our culture by Christian exclusivism might be to make this strongly worded statement: *Christianity is true, but that does not mean that Christians are right.* Indeed, because we believe that we are not saved through any capabilities of our own, but only through the gracious action of God, we ought to find it easy to admit that we often get things hopelessly wrong. If we were capable of being right, Jesus would not have needed to die for us.

And this initial statement begins the discussion of what I would identify as the next major problem that Christianity faces in our culture, and that is Christians. Because Christians have far too often bought into a belief that 'if Christianity is true then Christians are right', we have discredited our own faith. Christians are clearly as wrong as non-Christians about almost everything, and always have been. The Acts of the Apostles shows a very brief period where Christians were identifiable to the wider society around them by their distinctive lifestyle, but it instantly qualifies this with the story of Ananias and Sapphira (see Acts 4.32—5.11). In our society in Britain, Christians are, largely, indistinguishable from anyone else.[19] Some might wish to argue that that is because our society is founded upon Christian principles that allow us to live Christianly without even trying, but I'm afraid I don't believe that. I think it is much more likely that, in a society that still pays a surprising amount of lip-service to Christianity, many 'Christians' don't actually have to make any more radical commitment than the occasional Sunday attendance.

So if exclusivism is one problem that we face, the other is

that we can barely tell whether or not we are Christians. And if we can't, how could we expect others to? This is where the weakness that we identified in Robinson, in the lack of place given to the Christian community, really comes to the fore. Robinson was telling us more than he realized about British Christianity, and what is clear in the 1960s is just as clear now. Bonhoeffer wrote, fervently, about the role of discipleship in making Jesus Christ alive today, and that, I believe, is one of the central challenges facing Christians today. What does it mean to be a follower of Christ Jesus, and is it compatible with a comfortable, Western, middle-class, individualistic lifestyle? If not, do you still want to do it? Unless and until Christians honestly face that question, and allow it to change our lives, as it changed the lives of those disciples who followed Jesus on earth, no changes in liturgical language will ever make it clear to others what we believe about God.

When I was giving this paper as part of a dialogue at Southwark Cathedral, someone in the audience asked me a highly pertinent question. He asked, 'So are you saying that the answer to all our problems is to get everybody to go to church?'[20] Surely, he demanded, social action projects that actually took Christians out among the needy to demonstrate the love of God in action are actually more converting than a church full of people?

As I thought about the question afterwards, I realized that what it was pressing for was a new definition of 'church', or perhaps I mean an old one, that we have conveniently forgotten. The goal of Christian mission *is* to bring people into the Church, if the Church is defined as the body of Christ, the company of those who live in the life of the Spirit and share the communion of the Trinity. This whole-life definition of Church is not satisfied either by people who live God's life only on Sundays, or by those who show God's mercy but never introduce the needy to God himself. The goal is indeed to get everyone to go to church, but in doing so, church would have to change unimaginably, and many of its present occupants probably wouldn't like it.

Many Christians nowadays speak longingly of renewal, but the ones who seem convincingly renewed are the ones whose discipleship spills out of the church building.

Our culture has allowed us to believe that it is not a very difficult or challenging thing to be a Christian, and that it can be tagged on to our everyday lives. Being a Christian may provide you with some spiritual benefits, which are increasingly being recognized as psychologically and physiologically good for you. It may provide you with a circle of like-minded friends, but it is unlikely to demand anything too uncomfortable or embarrassing. Not Anglicanism, anyway.

But if I am suggesting that the call to discipleship is actually going to make huge demands on everyone, can I realistically expect that to be an attractive mission-statement – 'Join the church and life will get much harder'? Perhaps not, but if I am right in identifying lack of honesty as one of the major problems facing Christian mission today then, whatever other problems this may generate, it might at least begin to solve that one. It is bound to be true that some people will find the call to discipleship just too hard, and for them we trust to God's mercy and resourcefulness. We never hear the end of the story of the rich young ruler (see Mark 10.17ff.). Jesus instantly spots the one thing that the young man will find hard about the call – giving up his possessions. The last we see of him in Mark, he was 'shocked and went away grieving, for he had many possessions'.

Most missionary strategies have made demands for change and repentance for others, without showing any very great signs that we make the same demands upon ourselves. Radical discipleship, if practised by Christians, might not take away the difficulty of the exclusive claims we make about Christ, but it might at least demonstrate that we believe them to be true.

If I have correctly identified two of the most pressing problems facing twenty-first century British Anglicans – exclusivism and lack of commitment – what might be the theological outworkings of attempting to address these problems? Robinson began to attempt a theology to meet the objections he had identified. Can I do the same?

Change Your Life, Not the Words

The first and most basic change that is necessary will, I think, be obvious on the basis of what has been said above. And that is a change in the theology and practice of Church. Church – Christian community – Koinonia – call it what you will, is the most basic Christian unit. Not the individual, not the family, but the people of God. In order to make the church truly and effectively a place where discipleship is made real, churches need to be both smaller and bigger. I think there has to be a place for smaller community groups, a bit like house churches, where real intimacy and truthfulness is possible, and where nobody can be a passenger, because the gifts of all, however differently abled, are recognized as God-given. But I also think that churches need to be bigger. No one small group can think of itself as complete. All are bound to look outwards, and see their necessary interconnectedness.

This theology of the Church is not an arbitrary tool that we hope might work to bring more people to agree with us. It is an attempt to express, in lived form, something of our vision of God. The Christian understanding of God is that God is Trinity. The creative, life-giving force of the universe is not a solitary genius, but a social and loving community. If God is reality, then we cannot even approximate to reality on our own. We need each other if we are to have any sense of the life of God.

God's life, which we are attempting to explore and understand in our lives together, is a life that loves diversity. Father, Son and Holy Spirit are not interchangeable, but distinct, and their enjoyment of each other is so generous and appreciative that they long to share it even further. That is why we exist, because God genuinely enjoys what is not God, he makes room for it, gives it real freedom, and promises the fullness of divine life to it. So churches that are composed of people who are all alike, or who reject everything outside themselves or different from themselves are mirroring a warped understanding of the life of God.

That does not mean that we must be content with a good-natured and liberal 'live and let live' attitude to the world, because the Gospels suggest that this would actually be a 'live and let die' approach. God is the only source of life, and only connection with him brings life. What the incarnation makes clear is that connection with God does not mean the abandonment of what we really are. On the contrary, when God the Son comes to save, he saves us by perfecting what we actually are. The incarnation suggests that humanity is precisely the best vehicle for demonstrating the love of God.

Robinson rightly queries the homiletic usefulness of the Chalcedonian Definition of Jesus as both fully human and fully divine, but it might be that we too often give up on something that stretches our imagination to breaking point. All the best descriptions of reality actually do that. The concept of a black hole, for example, so full and dense that it is invisible? In fact, the Tillichian phrase, 'ground of our being', which Robinson takes up, is paraphrasing one of the insights that the Chalcedonian Definition assumes. We are created in the image of Christ, who comes in our image to show us ourselves. His is, indeed, the being on which ours is grounded. God embraces and enjoys what is not God, because he always has, and that is why he created in the first place. He draws us into his likeness, not to obliterate what we are, but because everything we are is hauntingly, tantalizingly, reminiscent of him in the first place, however much we have disguised that fact by living and believing that our life is our own, and not fed by the creator.

The definitions that Robinson rejected as 'frankly incredible' are perhaps so because they have been badly taught or misunderstood. Theologians like the Apostle Paul can bring them alive in, for example, talking about the relationship between our humanity and Christ's in terms of Adam and New Adam. This metaphor instantly connects God's initial creative activity, and his recreation in Christ. It makes clear both the likeness and the difference between us and Christ.

If this metaphor works less well in a culture where the Genesis creation story is not literally believed, one might look, instead, at the work of a modern theologian like Wolfhart Pannenberg. In his early masterpiece, *Jesus – God and Man*, Pannenberg argues that we have too often approached the problem of Christology in a way that is bound to make it incredible. We have started with two concepts – God and humanity – and a definition of each that makes them irreconcilable. But what if we start with the known quantity, the humanity of Jesus, and see what makes it unique? Pannenberg argues that Jesus is different from us only in being actually obedient to the God whom we call Father, and that this is how we can tell that he is God. His will and the will of the Father are united.[21]

It is possible, then, that the problem does not so much lie with the classical definitions of Christology and atonement in themselves, but with the poverty of our imaginations and our lives. If we see these things primarily as problematic 'theories', then that's what they will be.

But supposing we were to try to live as though, through the life of the Holy Spirit in us, our lives together as Christians could become the place where Jesus is present? Where Jesus is present, human life and the life of God are joined. Where Jesus is present, 'the poor hear good news, the captives are released, the blind see, the oppressed go free' (Luke 4.18, 19).

I am not suggesting that if we tried a bit harder, the Church could be full of perfect people. On the contrary, as I have already suggested, it is part of the self-definition of the Church that it is full of people who are fully aware of their imperfections, and their need of forgiveness. The Church is not the kingdom, but the presence of the Spirit makes it an appetizer. You should be able to get just a sniff or a glimmer of what the full glory of life in communion with God might be like.

All of this sounds very abstract and unlike the home life of our own dear church. The difference between the theory and the practice leads people in one of two directions. Some give up on 'the church', and try to live lives of social and political usefulness, in the belief that this is at least trying to follow the example of Jesus. This has much to commend it. As Moltmann has said, the trouble with the classical creeds is that they jump straight from the birth of Jesus to his death and resurrection, whereas his birth, death and resurrection only make any sense because of what he taught and did in between.[22]

The other possible reaction is to believe that God's work depends upon our purity and righteousness. This leads people increasingly to break ties with those with whom they disagree, and to become more and more churchy and inward-looking.

Both of these are lifestyles that make God incredible to those around us, because both actually rely wholly upon human action. The second may speak about God more, but it still assumes, just like the social action model, that we have to get it right, and that God is dependent upon us.

This appears, quite neatly, to let me off the hook of trying to suggest ways of redressing the situation, since that would again suggest that human action is the prerequisite. And, in a sense, that is true. God is God, with or without our help. But if God is the source of all reality, life and love, then it seems a pity not to take up his offer of being part of his life. What this Chapter is trying to suggest is that, if we try to be 'Honest to God' today, the onus lies fairly and squarely on

Christians actually to believe what they say they believe, and act as though they do – as best they can.

Robinson's central insight in his chapter on Christology is surely right. That Jesus 'brings God completely'. The problem is that, just as for many who encountered the human Jesus, so for us, God is sometimes a bit more than we actually want. And if that is the case, how can we possibly persuade others that they might want him? There is no one route to making ourselves better disciples, because there is no one point that is the universal sticking point for all Christians. But 'where your heart is, there will your treasure be also' (Matthew 6.21) is probably a good starting point.

I am not sure that Robinson's solutions to the problems he identified worked, though history suggests that they did not. I am reasonably confident that a Church full of disciples of Christ would. I'm just not very sure about how to get there. I hope God is.

Notes

1 J. A. T. Robinson, *Honest to God*, Westminster John Knox, 2002, p. 8.
2 The Greek word introduced into common Christian usage at the Council of Nicaea in 325 is *homoousios*. It was not a term familiar to most Christians, and it was not readily accepted, but is now accepted as a standard definition of the relationship between Father and Son.
3 See his generous tribute to those who defend the faith through 'fresh and intelligent' retelling of orthodoxy, Robinson, *Honest to God*, p. 7.
4 'the line to which I am referring runs right through the middle of myself', Robinson, *Honest to God*, p. 8.
5 See Robinson, *Honest to God*, Preface, p. 7.
6 He rejects this 'naturalism', which says that 'the divine is simply the human raised to the power of x', Robinson, *Honest to God*, p. 68.
7 Robinson, *Honest to God*, p. 78.
8 Robinson, *Honest to God*, p. 73.
9 Tillich quoted in Robinson, *Honest to God*, pp. 79 and 81. The italics are Robinson's.

10 Robinson, *Honest to God*, p. 182.

11 See, 'Theology through History', in David Ford (ed.), *The Modern Theologians*, 2nd edn, Blackwell, 1997, particularly p. 230.

12 See Herbert McCabe's contribution to David Edwards (ed.), *The Honest to God Debate*, SCM Press, 1963, pp. 166ff.

13 The other striking absence is the doctrine of the Trinity. Again, Robinson is quite typical of British theology in the 1960s in this omission. The huge growth in trinitarian studies in the last 20 years has made this a particularly glaring omission.

14 See Bethge's preface to the English edition, *Dietrich Bonhoeffer: A Biography*, Collins 1970, p. xx. Bethge clearly believed that Robinson and others had misinterpreted Bonhoeffer, on the basis of too little evidence.

15 'Who is Jesus Christ for us today?' is the question that Bonhoeffer pursued throughout his Christological writing.

16 Of course, I do not deny that there are those who find the whole idea of Christianity, from start to finish, incredible, and would argue their case in strongly rational terms. I do, however, believe that they are in a minority in a modern world that accepts all kinds of incomprehensible things.

17 J. Moltmann, *The Crucified God*, SCM, 1974, p. 160.

18 A good working definition for theologians can be found in Graham Ward's essay, 'Christianity and post-modernism', in Ford, *The Modern Theologians*.

19 Recent religious media coverage might suggest that Christians are, in fact, to be distinguished from others by their obsession with homosexuality.

20 I am very sorry that I cannot give credit where it is due, but I'm afraid I do not know the name of the man who asked this thought-provoking question. Nonetheless, I thank him.

21 See *Jesus – God and Man*, SCM, 1968, particularly Chapters 8 and 9.

22 See J. Moltmann, *The Way of Jesus Christ*, SCM, 1990, particularly Moltmann's suggested additions to the Creed on p. 150.

9. John Robinson:
A Memorial Sermon

ERIC JAMES

John would have approved my beginning this impossible sermon[1] with, not a text, but a passage, from the Epistle to the Ephesians, from the translation by his revered uncle Armitage, in his unsurpassed commentary:

> He gave some, apostles; and some, prophets; and some, evangelists; and some, pastors and teachers: for the perfecting of the saints for the work of ministry; for the building of the Body of Christ; till we all come to the unity of the faith and of the knowledge of the Son of God; to a perfect man, to the measure of the stature of the fullness of Christ: that we be no longer children, tossed to and fro and carried about with every wind of doctrine, by the sleight of men, by craftiness according to the wiles of error; but maintaining the truth in love, may grow up into Him in all things, which is the head, *even* Christ, from whom the whole body, fitly framed together and compacted by every joint of *its* supply, according to the effectual working in the measure of each several part, maketh the increase of the body, unto the building thereof, in love.[2]

I begin with that great passage for several reasons, but not least because that first phrase – 'He gave some, apostles; and some, prophets; and some, evangelists; and some, pastors and teachers' – makes it immediately clear what a superlatively gifted man John was – and I use the word literally; for to him it was given to be an apostle, and a prophet, and an evangelist; and a pastor, and a teacher – and many other gifts that are not contained in that great passage. But I begin with that passage primarily because it is in that context John's gifts, and indeed John's life, should be set; and it is in that context, certainly, John himself would have wanted them set.

That passage is above all about our human relating in and to the transcendent purpose of God: the End of all our relating. And that was the subject which possessed and held John all his life.

That so shy student, coming to Cambridge from Canterbury and Marlborough, having won a 'First' in the Theological Tripos at Jesus – and in 1941 the Burney Prize his uncle Forbes had won exactly 50 years before – took as the subject of his dissertation as Stanton Student here: 'Thou Who Art: The notion of personality and its relation to Christian theology, with particular reference to the contemporary I–Thou philosophy and the doctrine of the Trinity and the Person of Christ.' John's personal notebooks at the time confirm that he had been seized by the mystery of human relating. And, being John, that meant, in Barth's great phrase: 'taking rational trouble over the mystery'.

Barth, Buber, Brunner, Berdyaev, Kierkegaard, Macmurray – each made their contribution to John's first theological exploration – the first of many. 'Thou who art' was a conscious counter to Mascall's *'He Who Is': A Study in Traditional Theism*.[3] John was beginning as he meant to go on – 'questioning accepted doctrine, stripping away, getting to the heart, re-interpreting, constantly pushing out, being stretched, never resting content'.

Yet, even then, the rational Robinson knew that an intellectual approach was not enough. So when Mervyn Stockwood,

up from St Matthew's Moorfields, took a quiet day at Westcott,
John characteristically seized the initiative at the end of it, and
asked him if he would have him as his curate. For 17 years – in
Bristol, Cambridge and Southwark – John and Mervyn were
to work in close proximity and partnership; but it is difficult
to exaggerate the transformation that experience of community in the slums of Bristol effected in John. Bristol was to
John what Detroit had been to Niebuhr. Never could John
now imagine 'the building of the Body of Christ in love' to be
simply a spiritual and individual affair. He had been made to
realize that the building of the body, the call of the kingdom
and the claims of love must be responded to by the way of
social responsibility and answerability. There were things he
now knew God had to say to him that he could and would
hear only in and through the world of people. Not for the last
time God had forced John out into the world.

It was at this time John married Ruth, whom he had met
at Cambridge, and soon they started a family. John was
always – at least on the surface – nine parts of reason to one
of emotion. Each emotion had to force its way past the fierce
censor of reason. Yet, again, John's notebooks reveal what the
love of Ruth meant to him. Their marriage – like all the best
marriages – was unique – incomprehensible, often, of course
to outsiders; but to the two within, uniquely right, uniquely
blessed; both giving the other space; both reverencing their
differences as well as their affinities and sympathies. Neither
Ruth nor the children ever doubted John's love, though they
knew John was a husband and father unlike any other.

If at Bristol John's gift as pastor was most in evidence,
when, after three years, he went to Wells as chaplain to the
theological college, it was as pastor and teacher together that
he was most valued. And there, to theological exploration and
social answerability, he began to add the way of New Testament scholarship – that way, which, like the way of theological exploration, he knew meant for him 'digging to the roots,

probing, refusing to accept stock answers, returning to the source, compelling the Scriptures to yield up their message for today, going behind received interpretations, journeying to the centre'.

John never did better work than his first two studies – 'In the End God' and 'The Body'.[4] And never did he forsake those two subjects – not even at his own end. the Kingdom – the reign of God, realized but never wholly realized in this world – gripped him. So too did *The Body* – the body of Christ, the Church; the embodiment of God in 'the human form divine'; and the embodiment of the Christ in as many as receive him.

The basic work on those two studies had been done before John returned to Cambridge – to Clare – to eight happy years in a college which was proud of him, and understood him, and in which the threefold cord of friendship between John, as Fellow and Dean, and the Lady Margaret's Professor, Charlie Moule, and the chaplains – and *Liturgy Coming to Life*[5] – were the envy of many another college.

Those who had observed the three ways of theological exploration, biblical scholarship and social answerability that met in John – as he himself believed they did – were not surprised when he said 'Yes' to Mervyn Stockwood's invitation to go with him to Southwark, as Bishop of Woolwich. They knew that the pastor and teacher and scholar had it in him also to be apostle, and prophet and evangelist.

I can never myself forget Michaelmas Day 1959 – the day of John's consecration at Canterbury – and the poignant sight of the four young children in the front row of the congregation while Ruth lay in Hither Green hospital, 12 days after a severe cerebral haemorrhage, the future all unknown. Mercifully, she recovered to be the support of John for another quarter of a century.

Immediately John arrived in Southwark, he set to work on what is undoubtedly one of the most enduring testimonies to his ministry – the Southwark Ordination Course – that pioneer 'college without walls', 'for the perfecting of the saints for the work of ministry' – by which over 300 men and women have now been trained. It opened its doors within a year of John's arrival in Southwark – clear testimony to another of John's great gifts: the gift of administration. From the first, John's vision for the course was that it should train men and women, lay and ordained, and be fully ecumenical. It was to enable them to train for ministry without leaving their world: the world in which they lived and earned their living. It embodied John's idea of 'Doing Theology Today'.

The impact on John of the great secular desert of South London, with a population of a million and more, to most of whom the Church was massively irrelevant, was greater even than the impact of the slums of Bristol. Laid low with disc trouble – but out of anguish of heart and mind – John wrote *Honest to God*.[6] 'He gave some to be evangelists.' And *Honest to God* was supremely the work of an evangelist: of a missionary as passionately concerned with mission as St. Paul: mission to the secular city. For whatever reason, over one million people bought *Honest to God* – as you well know. No one can doubt it touched a nerve – no one, certainly, who has been allowed to read some of the correspondence – not only written at the time, but to John and to Ruth as John was nearing his death; letters that say things like: 'You helped me to believe again.' 'You helped me to pray again.' 'You made it possible for me to believe there was a place for me in the Church of God today.' Those letters I am glad to say, will be housed, at the invitation of the Archbishop of Canterbury, in the library at Lambeth, with all John's papers and many of his books.

Let it be said that never did John neglect his work as bishop because of *Honest to God* – in spite of a thousand letters in the first three months after its publication. He was always dropping in on the clergy and their families, and on the end of a telephone to them, and sending them postcards; and Ruth

and he would have them in droves to their home at Black-
heath. John had a remarkable ability to 'fill the unforgiving
minute', a power of concentration and a speed at working
which enabled him to demolish a pile of letters in no time, or
apply himself to the sermon to be prepared or to the book he
was reading – or writing. John never preached a dull sermon
in Southwark. Always there was something to arrest the
interest and sustain it. Who else would have preached – at
the institution of a vicar, to a church threatened with closure
– on the text: '"Behold, these three years I come seeking fruit
on this fig tree, and I find none: Cut it down; why cumbereth
it the ground?" And he answering said unto him, "Lord, let
it alone this year also, till I shall dig about it, and dung it:
and if it bear fruit, well; and if not, after that thou shalt cut
it down."'? Who else, being so shy and so lacking in small
talk, would have stood around so long chatting after institutions and confirmations – so that Bill Skelton – who had gone
from Clare to be Rector of Bermondsey when John went to
Woolwich – could say to me only a few days ago: 'When John
came to Bermondsey Parish Church the people adored him.'?
Cambridge, I think, has never quite realized and recognized
that John was a marvellous bishop and happy in his work.

But ten years in the episcopate – in the episcopate of
Woolwich – is a long time. Alas, the Church of England did
not know what to do with John. He suggested that he might
become a kind of 'bishop at large' – which is what Uncle
Armitage says the apostles were – roving missionaries. But
the idea of John 'let loose' was too much for those at the top.
'The bishop's role' John had written 'is to lead in setting men
free. And that means allowing them, for a start, really to see
that the Church has a greater investment in integrity than in
orthodoxy. Not without reason, men find this hard to believe.
But to attempt this very elemental liberation is something for
which I believe it has been worth trying to use the modest
opportunities that a bishopric provides in the modern world.'

In so doing, John became the best known bishop in the Church of God. But that only made him more of an embarrassment to the Church of England. F. A. Simpson used to say: 'The way they kill the prophets now is not by stoning but by consecrating them.' Consecration had not killed the gift of prophecy in John. He was a good prophet and a good bishop – indeed a superb prophet and a superb bishop – as all but a few of the clergy of the Diocese of Southwark at that time would gladly testify. The Church had therefore to resort to a more bland approach – at which it is not entirely unskilled.

It was suggested to John – and with good reason – that he had some big books of theology in him. He was pressed to return to Cambridge and to Trinity. Trinity has reason to be glad that eventually John more than willingly assented.

Back at Cambridge, John got on with his theology; but he had a stream of visitors from all round the world. Cambridge was never less of an ivory tower for a man than it was for John; and Trinity made it possible for him to make many a foray out into the world – to the United States, to South Africa, to South America, to India and Sri Lanka, to Australia and New Zealand. In *Truth is Two-eyed*,[7] John writes of the effortless superiority of people presuming like J. G. Frazer that one can write *The Golden Bough* without ever leaving Trinity Great Court! John did, of course, produce big books of theology here – notably the Hulsean Lectures *The Human Face of God*, *Redating the New Testament*[8] and the Bampton Lectures that – of his great kindness – Professor Moule delivered in Oxford. But the man who from the earliest days of his ministry had believed that whatever was 'headlines' that day was the raw material of theology – whether it was the Wolfenden Report, or the court case on Lawrence's *Lady Chatterley's Lover* – continued to 'do theology' that way in Cambridge, well realizing – perhaps sometimes too well realizing – that if you speak to the headlines you may yourself become headlines. So abortion, Apartheid, obscenity, the Falkland Islands, the nuclear bomb, the Turin Shroud and much else besides came within the compass of his critical concern.

Those whom he taught and to whom he was a pastor, and those who were aware how diligently and imaginatively he discharged his duties as Dean of Chapel – not least the successive chaplains of Trinity – had reason to be glad that the few years it had been suggested John should return to Cambridge eventually turned into 14. But some of us will be for ever ashamed that the Anglican Church never invited John to be the brilliant diocesan scholar-bishop he had it in him to be – in the steps of his masters Westcott and Lightfoot – or indeed to fill any further position of seniority.

There are some random thoughts, with which I must draw this – as I've said – impossible sermon to a close. John was in some ways an impossible man. Sometimes, I've no doubt, he must have seemed impossible to live with. But the gifts greatly outshone that impossibility. I can well remember times when I was with John – in Southwark, in the United States and here in Cambridge – the gauche, naïve side of him asserting itself. At such times you felt not only that you had to protect him from himself, but that it was a huge privilege to be allowed to do so. Sometimes it was like the privilege of looking after a child. But the exasperating moments were of such short duration; and it was never long before the glory of his gifts shone around.

There are three of those gifts to which I have not yet made reference.

I must pay tribute to John the writer. Honoured by his asking me to be his literary executor, I might nevertheless have had a hideous task before me, given John's huge output – but for his meticulous and detailed care in setting his things in order. To put it in a Johannine way: it is already clear that when the fragments that remain have been gathered up, that nothing be lost, there are likely to be several baskets that remain over and above with which John may yet feed and feast our minds.

You would also want me, I know, to pay tribute to John's

legendary courage in the last six months of his life – and to pay tribute to Ruth who in those months gave such 'priority to John'. But I would want to say that the courage of those last six months did but exemplify the courage *and faith* which John displayed all his ministry, as apostle, prophet, evangelist, pastor and scholar. And he who had *always* said: 'Your situation is the raw material of your theology' to the *end* made *his* situation the raw material of his theology.

Finally, I must pay tribute to John's gift of friendship – without which I would not be occupying this pulpit – which bears on its desk his initials. Never was there a more loyal friend than John. It was in our first meeting – in Clare, nearly 30 years ago – that John and I first talked together about friendship. We had met to talk about his Uncle Forbes' *Letters to Friends.*[9] Forbes was then to me the exemplar of all I believed about friendship. Little did I realize that his nephew would have so much to teach me – and, doubtless, to teach many another here today – about the gift of friendship.

Last August, when John's life was ebbing away, I went to Arncliffe to see him and Ruth in their Yorkshire village home. John was sitting in front of the television when I arrived, absorbed by the Kent versus Middlesex Cricket Final. We sat in virtual silence for a couple of hours. Towards the end of the match the light began to fail, so that the television cameras could scarcely pick up the players out on the field. Suddenly John turned to me with a wan smile – with I think some of his old delight in discovering a living figure of speech that he had, so to speak, plucked out of the air – and said: 'My life is rather like a limited over match, and the dusk is drawing on . . .'

In those last months, John was much drawn to the words of Henry Vaughan, which will shortly be sung as an anthem, in which the Body says:

Farewell: I goe to sleep; but when the day-star springs I'le wake agen.

John was as fond of that entry in Dag Hammarskjöld's *Markings*, which he made in 1953, when John was at Clare:

> – Night is drawing nigh –
> For all that has been – Thanks!
> To all that shall be – Yes![10]

And to God be the thanks and the glory for the life and the gifts of our brother John.

NOTES

1 Preached at the Memorial Service to Bishop John Robinson, Trinity College Chapel, Cambridge, 11 February 1984.
2 J. A. Robinson, *St Paul's Epistle to the Ephesians*, Macmillan, 1903, p. 95.
3 E. L. Mascall, *He Who Is. A study in traditional theism*, Longmans & Co., 1943.
4 *In the End, God . . . A study of the Christian doctrine of the last things*, James Clarke & Co., 1950; *The Body. A study in Pauline theology*, SCM Press, 1952.
5 *Liturgy Coming to Life*, A. R. Mowbray & Co., 1960.
6 *Honest to God*, SCM Press, 1963.
7 *Truth is Two-eyed*, SCM Press, 1979.
8 *The Human Face of God*, SCM Press, 1973; *Redating the New Testament*, SCM Press, 1976.
9 Forbes Robinson, *Letters to His Friends*, Spottiswoode, 1911.
10 Dag Hammarskjöld, *Markings*, Knopf, 1964, p. 89.